B

THIS A...

VOLUME TWO

LHP

THIS BOOK WAS PUBLISHED VIA AGREEMENT WITH
TOM PERRY'S LAUREL HILL PUBLISHING
ISBN: 9798861211604

Tom Perry's
Laurel Hill Publishing

LHP

Thomas D. "Tom" Perry   276-692-5300
4443 Ararat Highway   laurelhillpub@gmail.com
P O Box 11
Ararat VA 24053   https://squareup.com/store/
          laurel-hill-publishing-llc

Autographed copies available at https://
squareup.com/store/laurel-hill-publishing-llc
and
Available Tom Perry's Author Page on
Amazon at https://www.amazon.com/-/e/
B002F4UJGEA

I MUST CONTINUE. I CAN'T STOP NOW. I HAVE WRITING FEVER. GOOD OR BAD. THE FEVER IS BURNING ME MUCH AND I HAVE TO SPILL MY GUTS A LITTLE AT A TIME. AND BEFORE I DIE, I HAVE SEVERAL MORE CHAPTERS OF THINGS TO TELL, ABOUT MY ADVENTURES IN THE BAIL BONDS BUSINESS. SOME WERE VERY SERIOUS AND DANGEROUS. I COULD HAVE BEEN SERIOUSLY INJURED OR KILLED. SOME FUNNY AND SOME THAT JUST DOESN'T MAKE SENSE. I WILL STRIKE WHILE THE IRON IS HOT. AND AT MY AGE THE IRON COOLS OFF FAST. SOMETIMES I HAVE A MILLION MEMORIES RUNNING THROUGH MY MIND AND ALL AT THE SAME TIME.

AT THE LEAST, THIS AIN'T NO DOG.

MY HILLBILLYONTICS GETS CONFUSED AND CROSSED OVER WITH MY FORMER EDUCATION WHICH WAS TAUGHT TO ME IN A FORMER MANNER AND NOT IN HILLBILLYONTICS. THE WAY I WAS RAISED AND MY UPBRINGING WAS IN THE HILLBILLYONTICS STYLE. THIS WAS IN A SOMEWHAT COUNTRY MANNER. AND FOR ME TO WRITE BOOKS OF MY ADVENTURES AND LIFE HAPPENINGS, SEEMS TO BE THE WILDEST THING THAT ANYONE IN MY FAMILY WOULD HAVE DONE.

OUR MOTHERS, GRANDMOTHERS, WIFE'S, GIRLFRIENDS, CHILDREN, AUNTS AND OTHER IMPORTANT PEOPLE IN OUR LIVES THAT WERE FEMALES.

SERIOUSLY,

THIS AIN'T NO DOG.

WE WERE TAUGHT TO CALL THE ELDERS IN THE AREA WE WERE RAISED IN UNCLE OR AUNT NO MATTER WHETHER THEY WERE KIN TO US OR NOT. THIS WAS OUT OF DUE RESPECT. TO MIND WHAT OUR MOTHERS AND FATHERS TOLD US. TO TAKE YOUR HAT OFF AT THE TABLE, IN CHURCH, WHEN THE NATIONAL ANTHEM PLAYED, WHEN YOU ENTERED SOMEONE ELSE'S HOUSE, WHEN A FUNERAL WENT BY AND OTHER PLACES AT CERTAIN TIMES, AND BY ALL MEANS IN A COURTROOM. WE PULLED OUR VEHICLES TO THE SIDE OF THE ROAD AND WAITED UNTIL A FUNERAL PROCESSION DROVE PAST BEFORE WE DROVE ON. AND WE PLACED OUR RIGHT

HAND OVER OUR HEART OR SALUTED IF YOU WERE IN THE MILITARY OR LAW ENFORCEMENT WHEN THE NATIONAL ANTHEM WAS PLAYED.

THIS AIN'T NO DOG.

WE CARRIED WATER FROM A SPRING THAT SEEMED TO BE HALF A MILE AWAY, BUT IT WASN'T THAT FAR. WE HAD TO SCURRY THE TADPOLES, WATER SKIMMERS AND AN OCCASIONAL WATER SNAKE OUT OF THE WAY TO DIP THE WATER FROM THE SPRING INTO OUR BUCKETS. AT THE YOUNGEST AGE I CAN REMEMBER WE CARRIED ALL THE WATER WE USED FROM THIS SPRING UNTIL LATER WHEN DAD AND AN UNCLE WHO LIVED NEXT DOOR HAD A WELL DUG TO SUPPLY WATER FOR BOTH FAMILIES. WHEN WE CARRIED WATER FROM THE SPRING. WE HAD WASH PANS THAT WE WASHED UP IN (OUR FACE AND HANDS), BEFORE WE ATE BREAKFAST, DINNER, OR SUPPER.

AND DINNER WAS OUR MIDDAY MEAL NOT OUR EVENING MEAL, BECAUSE THAT WAS SUPPER.

WE ALL SHARED THE SAME WASH PAN AND THE SAME TOWEL. WE DIDN'T WORRY ABOUT ANY GERMS OR DIDN'T CARE ABOUT THEM, BECAUSE EVERYONE WAS KIN AND OR THE SAME AS KIN.

WATER WAS HEATED IN PANS ON A WOOD BURNING COOK STOVE FOR THE BATHWATER. ALL OF US KIDS TOOK A BATH EVERY SATURDAY NIGHT IN A NUMBER THREE WASH TUB (WHETHER WE NEEDED IT OR NOT(LOL). IT WAS JUST BIG ENOUGH TO GET INTO AND YOU WASHED YOUR BODY AND YOUR HAIR. I ALWAYS TRIED NOT TO BE THE LAST ONE IN THE TUB TO TAKE MY BATH, BECAUSE THE WATER GOT A LITTLE MURKY LOOKING AFTER A FEW TOOK THEIR BATHS. IF WE WANTED TO, WE COULD ALWAYS CARRY MORE WATER AND HEAT IT ON THE STOVE TO HAVE MORE BATH WATER, AND THAT WAS OUR CHOICE. IF THE WATER GOT TOO MURKY LOOKING, I WOULD CARRY AND HEAT MORE WATER. IT WAS A LOT OF EXTRA WORK TO DO THAT.

WOW, THIS AIN'T NO DOG.

DAD WAS DISABLED WITH HIS RIGHT LEG OFF WHICH HE LOST IN A COAL MINING ACCIDENT. HE ALSO HAD TROUBLE BREATHING WITH HIS LUNGS DETERIORATING FROM THE DUST HE BREATHED IN THE COAL MINES.

THE OPERATORS AND OWNERS OF THE COAL MINES DIDN'T SEEM TO CARE ABOUT HIM LOSING A LEG OR HIS LUNGS GOING BAD DUE TO THE DUST IN THE COAL MINES. THEY WOULD NOT MAKE HIM A LEG AFTER HE LOST HIS.

DAD WAS TOO PROUD TO ASK FOR HELP AND THERE WAS VERY LITTLE AVAILABLE AT THAT TIME. HE SAID WE WOULD HAVE TO MAKE IT ON OUR OWN. WE HAD A LARGE HILLSIDE GARDEN WHERE WE GREW A GREAT DEAL OF OUR FOOD. WE HAD A CELLAR WHERE WE KEPT MANY CANS OF VEGETABLES MOM CANNED TO FEED US THROUGH THE WINTER.

AS THE OLD SAYING WAS, WE EAT WHAT WE CAUGHT. IF WE CAUGHT FISH, WE EAT FISH. IF WE KILLED SQUIRRELS, RABBITS, DEER, GROUND HOGS OR ANYTHING THAT COULD BE EATEN

WE WORKED HARD TO HELP WITH THE FAMILY. SO, WE COULD HAVE FOOD TO EAT, A WARM HOUSE IN THE WINTER, A JOHNNYHOUSE TO GO TO WHEN WE NEEDED TO RELIEVE OURSELVES ONE WAY OR THE OTHER. OH, IF IT WAS A TWO HOLER PEOPLE WOULD SAY YOU WERE RICH, BUT THE FACT OF THE MATTER WAS, THERE WERE USUALLY SEVERAL IN THE FAMILY.

THERE WERE TEN CHILDREN IN OUR FAMILY PLUS MOM AND DAD BUT WE ONLY HAD A ONE HOLER. DAD SAID THAT YOU SHOULDN'T BE LOOKING AT THE OTHER PEOPLE'S BUSINESS. SO, WE JUST HAD TO WAIT OUR TURN OR GO TO THE WOODS. I REMEMBER MANY TIMES GOING TO THE WOODS, TO USE NATURES LEAVES AND THE LARGE GREEN LEAVES WERE ABUNDANT, BUT YOU HAD TO WATCH THE THREE LEAF PLANTS BECAUSE THEY WERE POISON IVY. IT WOULD BREAK YOU OUT IN AN IRRITABLE RASH ALL OVER YOUR BOTTOM THAT WOULD BURN TO HIGH HEAVEN. IT TOOK A WHILE TO GET OVER THIS ASSBURN.

HEY, THE JOHNNYHOUSE WASN'T NO DOG AND THIS AIN'T NO DOG.

To build the johnnyhouse it consisted of digging a hole about 6 or 8 foot deep and however wide you wanted it to be. Once you dug your hole you built a frame over the hole and walls and a roof over that. This was built with sawmill A ROUGH lumber, sawed at a local SAWMILL, THAT cost about $10 or $15 per enough boards to build a johnnyhouse and there was usually some of the lumber left which was used while building a smokehouse, hog pen or chicken house. There was always a use for the lumber.

You had to be careful when using lumber that had been used in a previous building which had been torn down for one reason or another. The reason for using caution around this lumber and or stepping on it was because many times the nails hadn't been pulled from the boards and when you would step on one of these nails it would go into your foot and even through your shoe and into your foot. I remember stepping on one of these nails and seeing that the nail come through my shoe and stuck out of the top. This was very painful and it hurt as it went through my shoe and through my foot and the only way to get it out of my foot was to hold the board down and physically pull the nail back through my foot and shoe.

After sticking a nail in your FOOT, the remedy was to soak it in a warm pan of Epson salts. This process was to draw the infection out of your FOOT.

When getting injured around the old hillside farm you used rude and crude things to doctor your injury. EPSON salts was used to heal a rusty nail that you stuck in your foot. This was a remedy to prevent gangrene from setting up in your foot or other parts of the body.

Black salve was used to help heal boils you may have as well as other sores on the body. Horse liniment was used to help relieve the aches and pains one had on different parts of the body. Many kinds of salves and

OTHER THINGS USED TO HELP HEAL AILMENTS OF THE BODY COULD BE ORDERED FROM WATKINS, BLARE AND OTHER MAIL ORDER CATALOGS AS WELL AS MOST COUNTRY STORES.

IF YOU WERE IN THE MEADOWS, FIELDS OR OTHER PLACES AROUND THE FARM AND STEPPED ON A NEST OF HORNETS, YELLOW JACKETS, HONEY BEES, BUMBLE BEES OR OTHER STINGING INSECTS AND SOMEONE WAS WITH YOU ALMOST IMMEDIATELY THEY WOULD TAKE THE TOBACCO JUICE CHAWED OUT OF THE TOBACCO FROM THEIR MOUTH AND BEGIN SQUEEZING AND RUBBING IT OVER THE STINGS OF THE BEES OR INSECTS. AND SOMETIMES HOLDING THE JUICY TOBACCO CUD ON THE STING.

IF YOU GOT A BAD CUT AND HAD SHEEP DIP WITH YOU AT THE BARN, YOU WOULD POUR THE SHEEP DIP ON THE CUT UNTIL YOU GOT HOME SO YOU COULD PUT MERCUROCHROME, IODINE OR METHYLATE ON THE INJURY, THAN PLACE PIECES OF AN OLD BED SHEET ON IT AND TIE STRIPS OF THE SHEET ON IT TO HOLD IT IN PLACE. SOMETIMES THE MEDICINE WAS SATURATED ALL OVER THE HOMEMADE BANDAGE TO MAKE SURE IT HAD PLENTY.

MANY REMEDIES WERE USED FOR INJURIES, SORES, AND SICKNESS WHEN I WAS A BOY. AND APPARENTLY, THEY WORKED OR AT LEAST THEY HELPED MOM, DAD AND TEN OF THEIR CHILDREN SURVIVE.

FOLKS USED LAUGHTER TO HELP A PERSON GET ALONE IN LIFE. (YOU COULD ALWAYS TELL WHO YOUR BEST FRIENDS WERE IF YOU GOT BIT IN THE BUTT BY A POISONOUS SNAKE WHILE OUT IN THE FIELDS OR WOODS. MY USED TO BE FRIEND AND I WERE MILES BACK IN THE HILLS DIGGING GINSENG ONE DAY WHEN I GOT INTO A NEST OF COPPERHEAD SNAKES AND ONE OF THEM BITE ME HARD RIGHT IN THE BUTTOCKS AND I WAS UNABLE TO WALK, SO THE USED BE FRIEND TOLD ME HE WOULDN'T BE ABLE TO CARRY ME OUT OF THE WOODS SO HE WOULD RUN AND GET A DOCTOR AND SEE WHAT HE SAID.

THE DOCTOR TOLD HIM TO CUT AN X WHERE THE SNAKE HAD BIT ME AND SUCK THE POISON OUT. AND AFTER A WHILE HE CAME BACK AND I ASK MY USED TO BE FRIEND

WHAT THE DOCTOR SAID AND HE SAID LOUD AND CLEAR YOU GOING TO DIE SUCKER.)

(HE WASN'T SUCKING NO POISON OUT OF THE BUTT)

INSIDE THE JOHNNYHOUSE YOU HAD TO HAVE BUILT UP SEATS WITH HOLES IN THEM BIG ENOUGH TO TAKE CARE OF BUSINESS BUT SMALL ENOUGH SO YOU WOULDN'T FALL IN. YOU ALSO HAD TO HAVE A DOOR GOING INTO IT WITH A WOODEN PADDLE ON THE INSIDE AND OUTSIDE. THAT WAY YOU COULD FASTEN IT WHILE YOU WERE INSIDE AND NOT TO SHOW YOUR BOTTOM WHILE USING IT.

THE PADDLE PLUS A HOOK ON THE OUTSIDE INDICATED WHETHER ANYONE WAS USING IT OR WHETHER IT WAS EMPTY.

THE JOB IS NEVER FINISHED UNTIL THE PAPERWORK IS DONE. AND THE PAPER TO WORK WITH THEN CONSISTED OF SEARS AND ROEBUCK CATALOG AS WELL AS OTHER CATALOGS, MAGAZINES, AND NEWSPAPERS. I WAS ABOUT SIXTEEN BEFORE WE FINALLY BUILT A BATHROOM, EQUIPPED IT WITH A COMMODE, SINK AND TUB. AND WE STARTED USING TOILET PAPER. GOODBYE TO SEARS AND ROEBUCK AND RASHES ON YOUR BOTTOM.

WE SIMPLY RAN A PIPE FROM THE BATHROOM TO THE JOHNNYHOUSE HOLE AND WATER FROM A SHALLOW WELL. WE LEFT THE JOHNNYHOUSE IN PLACE FOR A FEW YEARS JUST IN CASE. SOMETIMES THE JOHNNYHOUSE WAS REFERRED TO AS THAT LITTLE BROWN (SHACK) HOUSE OUT BACK. OR THAT LITTLE BROWN SHACK OUT BACK. AFTER A BIG SUNDAY DINNER IT WAS ALWAYS FULL FROM THE MANY PEOPLE WHO ATE WITH US.

I MANY TIMES HAD TO SETTLE FOR THE PART OF THE CHICKEN THAT WENT OVER THE FENCE LAST. I ALWAYS WANTED A CHICKEN DRUMSTICK BUT THAT WAS TAKEN BY THE VISITORS WHO ATE SUNDAY DINNERS WITH US. AND THESE FOLKS WERE SOME OF THE MOST WONDERFUL KINFOLK AND FRIENDS THAT EVER SET FOOT ON GOD'S EARTH. I CERTAINLY MISS THOSE DAYS AND THOSE PEOPLE.

THE JOHNNYHOUSE WAS ALWAYS A WELCOME SITE TO ALL WHO GOT THAT PAIN IN THEIR BUTT. YOU COULD CALL UPON THE JOHNNYHOUSE OUT BACK SOMETIMES KNOWN AS THE LITTLE BROWN SHACK OUT BACK, TO LIGHTEN YOUR LOAD AND TAKE THE STOMACH AND BUTT PAIN AWAY.

YOU'RE RIGHT THIS AIN'T NO DOG.

AS I GREW OLDER, I REALIZED THINGS WERE CHANGING TO FAST, TOO SOON AND TOO OFTEN. AND I MANY TIMES WILL SAY I'M FROM THE OLD SCHOOL. THIS REFERRING TO THE MANNERS FOLKS HAD AND DISPLAYED IN THE YEARS OF OUR PAST. WE ARE BECOMING IF NOT ALREADY THE RAT RACE WHERE WE DON'T RESPECT, DON'T CARE ABOUT, AND DON'T GIVE A RAT'S ASS WHAT HAPPENS TO OTHERS. SUCH A SAD DAY. I DOUBT IF WE EVER WILL REVERT BACK TO THE OLD WAYS, THE OLD DAYS, OR THE DAYS WHEN EVERYONE CARED ABOUT EACH OTHER WHILE TAKING TIME TO SHOW IT AND HELP ONE ANOTHER.

"BIG JIM SAID WELL THE GOOD NEWS IS THAT THE RAT RACE IS OVER, AND THE BAD NEWS IS THE RATS WON."

THAT IS THOUGHTS AND NEEDS OF MYSELF IN THE FUTURE, TODAY AND THE PAST. I SEE NOTHING WRONG WITH EXERTING YOURSELF AND EXPRESSING YOURSELF AS TO WHERE YOU ARE GOING, WHERE YOU ARE AND WHERE YOU HAVE BEEN. THESE WERE SOME OF THE TRAITS OF THE PAST AND THE HILLBILLY WAYS. BLESS THE PEOPLE WHO LIVED AND SURVIVED THE HARD LIFE WE HAD TO LIVE IN.

BUT YOU KNOW WE WERE AS HAPPY THAN AS IF WE HAD GOOD SENSE. LOL. WE WERE POOR BUT WE DIDN'T KNOW IT, PROUD OF OUR AREAS WHERE WE LIVED WITH OURSELVES AND OUR NEIGHBORS. WE LOVED AND CARED ABOUT EVERYONE. YES, WE ARE HILLBILLYS AND OUR WAY OF LIFE IS SOMEWHAT DIFFERENT FROM OTHER FOLKS IN THE WORLD OR COME TO THINK ABOUT IT MAYBE FOLKS IN THE OTHER PARTS OF THE WORLD'S WAYS ARE DIFFERENT FROM OURS. THINK ABOUT IT!

AND NOW I WILL BEGIN TELLING ABOUT MORE OF MY ADVENTURES IN THE BAIL BONDS BUSINESS. SOMETIMES RAMBLING ON IS A PART OF LIFE, ESPECIALLY WHEN YOU GET OLD. HOLD ON TO YOUR HAT OR WHATEVER YOU FEEL IS MOST IMPORTANT TO HOLD ONTO. YOU COULD ORDER A 303 BRITISH END FIELD RIFLE FOR $1.1/2. OR ANOTHER KIND OF RIFLE OR SHOTGUN FOR SEVENTY FIFE CENTS OR $1.00. ALSO, YOU COULD ORDER OTHER KINDS OF GUNS OR KNIVES OR WEAPONS FOR LITTLE OR VERY LITTLE. JUST ORDER THROUGH THE MAIL, WITH A ½ CENT STAMP ANYTHING YOU WANTED TO BUY YOU COULD ORDER FROM ONE OF THE MANY CATALOGS. ANYTHING YOU WANTED TO LOOK AT YOU COULD SEE IN ONE OF THE CATALOGS. ALL YOU HAD TO DO WAS ORDER FROM A CATALOG AND IT WOULD ARRIVE IN A WEEK OR TWO.

THIS JOHNNYHOUSE WAS A COMFORT TO ALL.

NO DOG.

I COULD NOT OMIT THIS CHAPTER IN THIS BOOK, BECAUSE THAT IS WHEN I LOST MY MOST PRECIOUS POSSESSION ON EARTH. THE ONE I LIVED FOR AND WOULD HAVE DIED FOR.

SHE WAS MY SOUL COMPANION, MY LOVE, THE REASON MY HEART KEPT BEATING, THE ONE WHO COMFORTED ME WHEN I WAS DOWN, WHEN I NEEDED A MORAL BOOST, WHEN I WAS SICK, SHE WAS ALWAYS BY MY SIDE. SHE WAS THE MOST WONDERFUL HOUSEKEEPER IN THE WORLD. SHE MADE SURE I WAS ALWAYS WELL DRESSED. SHE NEVER LET ME WEAR ANYTHING UNTIL SHE IRONED IT AND MADE SURE IT WAS IN GOOD SHAPE. SHE WAS PROUD OF ME AND LOVED ME AND I WAS HER AS WELL. I DIDN'T HAVE TO WORRY ABOUT SHOPPING FOR CLOTHING, FOOD OR ANYTHING AND EVERYTHING WE NEEDED. WE WERE FORTUNATE ENOUGH TO BE ABLE TO GO PLACES AND DO THINGS TOGETHER AND I'M SO THANKFUL FOR THAT. THOSE MEMORIES AND OTHERS IS ALL I HAVE LEFT OF HER. MAY OUR HEAVENLY FATHER ALLOW ME TO KEEP THOSE AND OTHER MEMORIES UNTIL I DIE.

SHE WAS AN EXCELLENT COOK WHO ALWAYS MADE SURE I HAD WONDERFUL MEALS TO EAT AT ALL TIMES. ANYTHING I VENTURED INTO IN LIFE SHE WAS

ALWAYS VERY SUPPORTIVE OF ME AND RIGHT BY MY SIDE AT ALL TIMES HELPING ME ACHIEVE IN BUSINESS AND IN LIFE. IT SEEMS SHE WANTED TO PARTICIPATE IN EVERYTHING, AND WHAT A BLESSING THAT WAS TO ME.

AT TIMES WHEN SHE WAS IN THE HOSPITAL OVERNIGHT OR SEVERAL DAYS I WAS ALWAYS AT HER SIDE WITH HER, AND SHE WAS ALWAYS AT MY SIDE WHEN I WAS SICK OR IN THE HOSPITAL. WE HAD NO ONE ELSE JUST EACH OTHER.

MY CHILDREN DIDN'T SEEM TO CARE ABOUT ME, AND HER SON NEVER CARED ABOUT HER. HE NEVER STAYED OR OFFERED TO STAY EVEN ONCE IN THE HOSPITAL WITH HIS MOTHER. AND THIS INCLUDED OVER 30 TIMES SHE WAS IN THE HOSPITAL OVER THE YEARS WITH HER HEART PROBLEMS AND OTHER HEALTH ISSUES. HE JUST WANTED AND RECEIVED HER THINGS INCLUDING MUCH MONEY BEFORE AND WHEN SHE PASSED AWAY.

LORD I HUMBLY COME TO YOU TO THANK YOU FOR THE WONDERFUL YEARS OF LOVING EACH OTHER SO TRULY. I KNOW THAT WITHOUT YOU IT COULD NOT HAVE HAPPENED. BUT LORD GOD I NEED HER SO BADLY NOW THAT SOMETIMES I CAN'T SLEEP, EAT OR EVEN THINK CLEARLY WITHOUT HER. WHEN I LOOK AROUND ME LORD I SEE EMPTINESS EVERYWHERE BECAUSE SHE'S NOT THERE. LORD I THINK SOMETIMES WHY DID YOU NOT TAKE ME, INSTEAD OF HER. SHE WAS THE GOOD ONE, THE ANGEL. THE ONE WHO HELD MY HEART. I DEPENDED ON HER FOR MOST EVERYTHING, AND SHE DID ME.

I HURT SO BAD THAT I CAN'T DO ANYTHING WITHOUT HER. WHILE SITTING HERE WRITING ABOUT HER THE TEARS HAVEN'T STOPPED POURING FROM MY EYES. I COULD HAVE FILLED BUCKETS FULL OF TEARS. HOW CAN AND WHY DOES THIS HURT SO MUCH.

I HAVE LOST KINFOLKS OVER THE YEARS BUT IT HASN'T TORN AT MY HEART AND SOUL AS BAD AS LOOSING MILLIE. AFTER BEING TOGETHER FOR OVER 30 SOME YEARS. IF TIME HEALS ALL IN MEN AND MICE, THAN IT WILL BE AT THE TIME OF MY DEATH WHEN I HAVE SOULFUL RELIEF, AND THIS WILL BE WHEN OUR SOULS MEET AND ARE TOGETHER IN SPIRIT WHILE THE AGES ROLL ON AND ON, AMEN.

I WILL ALWAYS HAVE A DEEP BURNING HURT IN MY HEART AND MY SOUL WHILE MISSING HER SOOTHING WORDS AND SUPPORTIVE ACTIONS. SHE COULD MELT THE COLDEST SNOW WITH HER COMFORT AND LOVE SHE GAVE ME. WHAT IN THIS WORLD WILL I EVER DO WITHOUT HER? I ASK GOD WHY DIDN'T HE TAKE ME INSTEAD OF HER AND ALL I COULD EVER THINK WAS HE NEEDED ANOTHER ANGEL IN HEAVEN. IT'S STILL HARD TO ACCEPT AND I CRY WHEN I THINK ABOUT MY LOSS. I THINK SHE IS SMILING DOWN AT ME WHILE SAYING PLEASE DON'T CRY IT WILL BE O K UNTIL WE MEET AGAIN. AND EVEN WITH HER SAYING THAT I CAN'T CONTROL MY EMOTIONS WHEN I THINK ABOUT THE GOOD TIMES AND BAD THAT WE WENT THROUGH IN OUR TIMES WE WERE TOGETHER HERE ON EARTH.

I MUST PAY A VERY HUMBLE TRIBUTE TO THE MOST WONDERFUL WOMAN WHO EVER LIVED. I AM SO PROUD I CAN SAY I HAD THIS LADY IN MY LIFE FOR OVER 30 YEARS. I TELL HER I LOVE HER IN MY PRAYERS EACH NIGHT AND SOMETIMES DURING THE DAY. MILLIE SUE SPARKS WILL LIVE ON IN MY MEMORIES FOREVER. AND MOST EVERYONE WHO EVER MET MILLIE WOULD SAY THE SAME. WE DID EVERYTHING TOGETHER. IF I STARTED A DIFFERENT BUSINESS OR ADVENTURE, SHE WOULD JOIN ME WHILE HELPING ME IN EVERY WAY SHE COULD. IF SHE WAS ONLY HERE NOW TO COMFORT ME AND SHELTER ME FROM THE TERRIBLE HURT, I HAVE WHILE LOSING HER AND MISSING HER SHOWER OF LOVE SHE ALWAYS HAD FOR ME.

REST IN PEACE MY LOVE UNTIL I CAN BE WITH YOU ONCE MORE AND WE CAN WALK IN HEAVEN TOGETHER AND STROLL THROUGH AND DOWN THOSE PEARLY STREETS MADE OF GOLD, AND OUR HEALTH AND DISABILITIES WILL NOT BE A FACTOR TO EITHER OF US. THAT IS SUCH A WONDERFUL THOUGHT TO ME BECAUSE I'M HAVING SUCH A HARD TIME HERE WITHOUT HER. IF I DIE TOMORROW OR EVEN RIGHT NOW IT WANT BE SOON ENOUGH TO BE CLOSE TO HER AGAIN SO I CAN TELL HER I LOVE HER JUST ONE MORE TIME.

NO ONE COULD HAVE EVER TOLD ME HOW BAD I WOULD HURT WITHOUT HER. I TRY TO PLACE MY MIND SOMEWHERE ELSE TO KEEP FROM THINKING ABOUT HER LOSS TO ME. I WILL NEVER SEE HAPPINESS AGAIN IN MY LIFE. LORD, PLEASE I PRAY TO YOU TO KEEP HER SAFE UNTIL I GET THERE TO TAKE OVER THE JOB OF

KEEPING HER FROM ALL HARM WHILE THE AGES ROLL ON AND UNTIL WE ARE IN HEAVEN TOGETHER FOREVER. AMEN.

THIS AIN'T NO DOG

I SIT HERE THINKING ABOUT DIFFERENT THINGS THAT HAPPENED TO ME AND OTHERS IN THE BAIL BONDS BUSINESS. I REMEMBER WHEN THE CIRCUIT COURT JUDGE IN A JUDICIAL CIRCUIT, WAS MORE OR LESS THE BOSS OVER THE MAGISTRATES IN HIS JUDICIAL CIRCUIT. THE JUDGE WOULD PLACE CONDITIONS ON THE DEFENDANT THAT HE WAS SUPPOSED TO ABIDE BY WHEN RELEASED ON BOND. I OBSERVED JUDGES ORDERING THAT THE DEFENDANT COULD ONLY BE RELEASED ON BOND WHEN CASH WAS PLACED AS COLLATERAL, OR SOMETIMES REAL ESTATE AND OR SOMETIMES WHILE USING A BAIL BONDSMAN.

THIS AIN'T NO DOG.

NO JUDGE HAD A LEGAL RIGHT TO ORDER THAT ONLY ONE OR MORE OF THESE COULD BE USED WHILE DOING THE BOND. THE TEN AMENDMENTS TO THE CONSTITUTION IN THE 8TH AMENDMENT STATES FAIR BAIL AND IMPLIES THAT EITHER CASH, REAL ESTATE AND OR A BAIL BONDSMAN COULD BE USED TO PROCURE THE BAIL OF A DEFENDANT, AND NOT JUST ONE OR THE OTHER.

IT SEEMS THAT THE JUDGES WERE TRYING TO DICTATE TO THE MAGISTRATES THAT THEY WANTED THE BOND DONE IN A MANNER WHICH WASN'T IN TRUE LEGAL FORM. AND A FEW MAGISTRATES STOOD UP TO THESE JUDGES AND TOLD THEM THE PROPER WAY THE BOND COULD BE DONE WHILE THE JUDGES BACKED DOWN AND ABANDONED THEIR DEMANDS THEY WERE ILLEGALLY TRYING TO PLACE ON THE CONDITIONS OF BAIL OF A DEFENDANT. ALTHOUGH MOST OF THE MAGISTRATES WERE AFRAID AND DIDN'T WANT TO GO UP AGAINST A JUDGE.

MY FIRST RECOLLECTION OF A MAGISTRATE STANDING UP AGAINST A JUDGE WAS IN TAZEWELL COUNTY VIRGINIA. THE JUDGE HAD PLACED A CONDITION OF BOND THAT IT HAD TO BE DONE WITH CASH ONLY. THE MAGISTRATE ALLOWED THE BOND TO BE DONE THROUGH A BONDSMAN. I WAS THE BONDSMAN. WHEN THE

MAGISTRATE STOOD UP AGAINST THE WRONGFUL DEMANDS OF THE SAME SAID JUDGE HE BACKED DOWN AND CONFORMED TO THE 8TH AMENDMENT AND ITS MEANING THAT A DEFENDANT HAD A RIGHT TO USE ANY OF THE ALLOWED TO PROCURE THEIR BOND.

ANOTHER MAGISTRATE IN THE OFFICE TOLD HER SHE WOULD HAVE THE JUDGE TO THROW A FIT ON HER IF SHE DID NOT COMPLY WITH THE JUDGE'S ORDERS. THE MAGISTRATE THAT DONE THE BOND ALLOWING A BONDSMAN TO USE OTHER THAN WHAT THE JUDGE HAD ORDERED STATED THAT A JUDGE DID NOT HAVE THE RIGHT TO PLACE SUCH A CONDITION ON A DEFENDANT AND SHE POINTED OUT THE 8TH AMENDMENT. THE JUDGE CALLED HER THE NEXT DAY TO COMPLAIN AND SHE LET HIM HAVE IT WHILE POINTING OUT THE 8TH AMENDMENT TO HIM. AND WHEN SHE DID, HE SHUT UP AND APOLOGIZED TO HER. THAT WAS A REAL EXPERIENCE TO OBSERVE A JUDGE APOLOGIZE TO A MAGISTRATE FOR HIS MISTAKE AND ERRORS.

IF A JUDGE PLACED A CONDITION OF BOND ON A DEFENDANT YOU DIDN'T HEAR THE PROSECUTING ATTORNEY SAY ANYTHING WHETHER IT WAS LEGAL AND COMPLIED WITH THE CONSTITUTION OR NOT. OCCASIONALLY YOU WOULD FIND THE DEFENDANT'S ATTORNEY CHALLENGING A BOND CONDITION. THIS WAS DONE MOSTLY IF THE DEFENDANT HAD A JOB AND NEEDED TO TRAVEL OUTSIDE THE PERIMETERS SET BY THE JUDGE, AND MOST OF THE TIME THE JUDGE WOULD CHANGE THE CONDITIONS SO THE DEFENDANT COULD TRAVEL TO WORK.

THIS AIN'T NO DOG.

ONCE I BONDED THREE PEOPLE OUT OF JAIL THAT HAD THE SAME CHARGES AGAINST THEM. POSSESSION OF DRUGS, WITH INTENT TO DISTRIBUTE. THE BONDS TOTALED $9,000. THAT AMOUNTED TO OVER $3,000 PER EACH PERSON. THE DEFENDANTS WERE ALL RELATED. THE HUSBAND, HIS WIFE, AND HIS SISTER. THE MAN AND THE WOMEN SEEMED TO BE O K PEOPLE WHO WOULD SHOW FOR COURT AND FACE THEIR FATE WITH THE JUDGE UPON A WHEN I DID THE BOND. BOY WAS I WRONG. THE PRESIDING JUDGE AT THEIR BOND HEARING HAD PLACED AN ORDER ON EACH OF THEM STATING THEY COULD NOT LEAVE THE STATE OF VIRGINIA UNTIL

AFTER THE CASE AGAINST THEM WAS FINISHED AND ALL THEIR SENTENCING WAS COMPLETED. WELL, THEY DIDN'T COMPLY WITH THE JUDGE'S ORDERS.

THIS WAS SOME BULL CRAP WHEN THEY DIDN'T DO WHAT THE JUDGE SAID, BUT"

THIS AIN'T NO DOG.

AFTER A MONTH OR SO I RECEIVED A SHOWCAUSE TO COME TO COURT AND TELL THE JUDGE WHY THEY DIDN'T SHOW FOR COURT AND WHERE THEY WERE. WELL, I DIDN'T HAVE A CLUE WHERE THEY WERE AT THAT TIME. SO, THE ONLY THING I COULD TELL THE JUDGE WAS I DIDN'T KNOW WHERE THEY WERE OR WHY THEY DIDN'T SHOW FOR COURT. I TOLD HIM I HAD BEEN LOOKING FOR THEM EVERYWHERE I THOUGHT THEY MAY BE. BUT THAT DIDN'T SATISFY THE GRUMPY ASS JUDGE WHO WAS SUBSTITUTING FOR THE REGULAR JUDGE. THE REGULAR JUDGE WHO WAS USUALLY IN THIS COURT WAS NOT THERE DUE TO SICKNESS IN HIS FAMILY. I WISH HE HAD BEEN THERE BECAUSE THE STAND IN JUDGE GAVE ME ONLY 30 DAYS TO FIND THE DEFENDANTS OR PAY A FORFEITURE OF $9,000. THE SAME AS WHAT THE BOND WAS. IF THE REGULAR JUDGE HAD BEEN THERE, I'M SURE HE WOULD HAVE ASKED ME HOW MUCH TIME I NEEDED TO FIND THEM. I PROBABLY WOULD HAVE ASKED HIM TO GIVE ME 90 DAYS AND I'M SURE HE WOULD HAVE. BUT IF A FROG HAD WINGS, HE WOULDN'T BUMP HIS ASS, SO IF I ONLY HAVE 30 DAYS TO FIND THEM, I HAD TO GET BUSY DOING SO.

I KNOW THIS AIN'T NO DOG.

ONE THING ABOUT IT, YOU HAD TO COMPLY WITH THE ORDERS OF THE JUDGE SITTING ON THE BENCH. YOU COULD APPEAL WHAT THE JUDGE ON THE BENCH SAID AND GO TO A HIGHER COURT, BUT THAT COST MONEY AND, I DIDN'T LIKE THE JUDGE OF THE HIGHER COURT. HE DRANK HIS LUNCH (BEER AND WHISKEY) AND PASSED JUDGEMENT ON PEOPLE FOR THE SAME THING HE DID.

THE CIRCUIT COURT JUDGE AT THAT TIME WAS A REAL ASSHOLE. HE GOT CAUGHT IN ANOTHER STATE DRIVING DRUNK WHEN HE WRECKED HIS CAR. I DON'T KNOW IF HE WAS CROSS DRESSING, OR NOT, BUT THEY SAID HE WAS. AND THE POLICE WHO

ARRESTED HIM DIDN'T KNOW WHO HE WAS SINCE THEY WERE IN WEST VIRGINIA WHEN THE DRIVING DRUNK AND OTHER HAPPENED. THEY PROBABLY WOULD HAVE TAKEN HIM HOME AND NOT HAVE ARRESTED HIM IF THEY KNEW HE WAS A CIRCUIT COURT JUDGE. SUPPOSABLY, HE HAD BEEN TO A CLUB AND WAS GOING HOME.

WELL AS LUCK WOULD HAVE IT (I LIKED IT) THE NEWSPAPERS GOT A HOLD OF THIS AND THE POLICE FOUND THEMSELVES IN A POSITION WHERE THEY HAD TO CHARGE HIM. I'M SURE THE PUBLIC WOULD HAVE BEEN OUTRAGED IF THEY HAD LET HIM GO.

HEY, HEY THIS AIN'T NO DOG TODAY.

BUT EVEN AT THAT THE JUDGE ON THE BENCH AT THAT TIME GAVE HIM SUCH A LIGHT SENTENCE THAT IT WAS NOT JUSTIFIABLE. THIS WAS IN WEST VIRGINIA; A BORDERING STATE AND I GUESS THIS IS WHAT MANY PEOPLE WOULD CALL PROFESSIONAL COURTESY. AND I DIDN'T AGREE WITH IT AT ALL. HE HAD TO SPEND FOUR HOURS A DAY FOR TWO DAYS IN THE CLERK'S OFFICE AND THAT WAS HIS SENTENCE FOR HIS CRIMINAL ACTS. MANY PEOPLE WERE UPSET WITH THIS LIKE NOTHING SENTENCE, BUT NOTHING COULD BE DONE ABOUT IT. BUT IN REVENGE FOR HIS ACTS MYSELF AND MANY OTHERS WROTE J E R K. JUDICIAL ELECTORAL REVIEW COMMITTEE. AND THIS COMMITTEE OVERSEEN THE JUDGES DEMEANOR AND ACTIONS IN COURT. VA IS ONE OF ONLY A FEW STATES THAT APPOINT THE JUDGES. MOST STATES ALLOW VOTERS TO ELECT THE JUDGES. UPON LEARNING FROM SEVERAL PEOPLE OF THE JUDGE'S CRIMINAL ACTS AND DEMEANOR THEY REMOVED HIM FROM THE BENCH. (GOOD RIDDANCE).

THIS AIN'T NO DOG

NO JUDGE OR JUDICIAL OFFICIAL IS ABOVE THE LAW AND SHOULD BE PUNISHED FOR THEIR CRIMINAL ACTIONS THE SAME AS ANY CITIZEN. AND THAT GOES FOR ANY, AND ALL POLITICIANS WHO ARE SUPPOSED TO BE REPRESENTING CITIZENS FAIRLY AND RESPONSIBLY AND IF THEY DON'T, THEY SHOULD BE PUNISHED AS WELL.

NO MISTREATMENT OF CITIZENS SHOULD EVER OCCUR FROM ANY OFFICIAL WHO IS SUPPOSED TO BE WORKING FOR THE BETTERMENT OF THE PEOPLE. THIS NEVER SHOULD BE THE WAY CITIZENS ARE TREATED AND.

THIS AIN'T NO DOG.

WELL, I GOT TO GET BACK TO THE THREE PEOPLE I BONDED OUT WHO DIDN'T SHOW FOR COURT. I DID SEVERAL SURPRISE VISITS TO THEIR HOME, THEIR UNCLE'S HOME AND OTHER FOLKS WHO KNEW THEM. THIS WAS WITHOUT SUCCESS. SO, I WAS ABLE TO FIND OUT ABOUT SOME OF THEIR KIN FOLKS WHO LIVED IN WASHINGTON STATE.

AS I ATTEMPTED TO FIND OUT MORE INFORMATION, I WAS ABLE TO GET THE PHONE NUMBER OF THE SHERIFF'S OFFICE IN THAT AREA. SO, I CALLED THE SHERIFF, TOLD HIM WHO I WAS AND ASK HIM IF HE HAD ANY INFORMATION ON THESE THREE SKIPS I WAS LOOKING FOR. AND JUST AS LUCK WOULD HAVE IT, HE SAID YES, I KNOW ABOUT THESE THREE AND I JUST HAPPEN TO HAVE THEM IN MY HOTEL. I COULD HAVE DANCED ON WATER WHEN I HEARD HIM SAY THIS. AND I ASK HIM IF HE COULD HOLD THEM FOR ME., HE SAID ANYTHING LIKE THAT HAD TO BE APPROVED BY THEIR JUDGE BUT HE SAID HE DIDN'T SEE A PROBLEM WITH THAT.

THIS AIN'T NO DOG BUT IT'S A GOOD DOG.

THE NEXT DAY I WAS ABLE TO TALK TO THE LOCAL JUDGE IN THAT AREA. HE TALKED AS COMMON AS I DO AND SEEMED TO BE A FRIENDLY OLE CUSS. HE SAID, I HEAR YOU WOULD LIKE ME TO HOLD SOME OF OUR JAIL CITIZENS UNTIL YOU CAN GET HERE TO PICK THEM UP. I SAID YES, YOUR HONOR I WOULD APPRECIATE IT IF YOU WOULD. HE SAID I'LL HOLD THEM FOR YOU UNTIL YOU GET HERE. I TOLD HIM HOW MUCH THAT MEANT TO ME FOR HIS ASSISTANCE. HE SAID DON'T WORRY THEY WILL BE HERE WAITING ON YOU. WE HAD AN OLE BOY CONVERSATION AND I THANKED HIM AGAIN. THIS WAS WHAT I WAS LOOKING FOR, AND NOW I HAD TO MAKE ARRANGEMENTS TO GO GET THEM BECAUSE TIME WAS RUNNING OUT UNTIL I WOULD HAVE TO PAY THE BOND. THIS AIN'T NO DOG, BUT IT WAS AGGRAVATING

THINKING I MAY HAVE TO PAY THE $8,000 FORFEITURE FOR THE BOND PLUS THE COURT APPEARANCES AND OTHER EXPENSES.

THAT SAME EVENING. I TALKED TO ONE OF MY BAIL BONDS SUB-AGENTS WHO WORKED FOR ME, I ASKED HIM ABOUT GOING TO GET THEM. HE SAID HE WOULD GO IF SOMEONE WOULD GO WITH HIM. HE HAD THE POWERS TO REARREST A DEFENDANT BAIL SKIP AND THAT THE AUTHORITY WAS GRANTED BY ME THE BONDSMAN WHO HAD BONDED THE DEFENDANTS OUT OF JAIL. HE SAID HE KNEW SOMEONE WHO WOULD PROBABLY GO WITH HIM, AND HE WOULD LET ME KNOW THAT NIGHT IF THEY WOULD GO.

MY AGENT CALLED ME THAT NIGHT AND SAID THE FELLOW WOULD GO WITH HIM. THEN CAME THE PART OF HOW MUCH MONEY I WOULD PAY THEM. THEY WOULD HAVE TO DRIVE THREE DAYS AND THREE NIGHTS TO GET THERE AND THE SAME AMOUNT OF TIME TO GET BACK. SO, I ASK HIM HOW MUCH HE WOULD TAKE TO GO GET THEM AND BRING THEM BACK TO THE JAIL. HE SAID IF I WOULD PAY FOR THEIR MEALS, HE WOULD DO IT FOR $2,500. THIS WOULD SAVE ME A LOT OF MONEY BY DRIVING INSTEAD OF FLYING, SO I TOLD THEM TO GO AS SOON AS THEY COULD.

TO FLY MY AGENTS OUT TO WASHINGTON STATE AND GET THE THREE SKIPS AND BRING THEM BACK TO VIRGINIA WOULD HAVE COST ME $9,500, THEREFORE I SAVED MONEY BY ALLOWING MY BAIL AGENT TO DRIVE OUT AND GET THEM. AND I PAID FOR THEIR MEALS. THERE WERE NO HOTEL EXPENSES BECAUSE ONE OF THEM SLEPT WHILE THE OTHER DROVE.

ALSO, TO FLY WITH PEOPLE YOU HAVE DETAINED YOU HAD TO SHOW THE REASON YOU HAD THEM DETAINED. AND YOU HAD TO HAVE DOCUMENTATION THAT YOU WERE NOT KIDNAPING THESE PEOPLE AND YOU HAD THE AUTHORITY TO REARREST THEM. AND YOU HAD TO HAVE ONE ON ONE. IN OTHER WORDS, THERE HAD TO BE ONE PERSON FOR EVERY PERSON YOU HAD DETAINED. I GUESS IT WOULD COST SEVERAL THOUSAND MORE TO FLY DETAINED PEOPLE IN TODAY'S WORLD EVEN IF YOU COULD DO SO WITH ALL THE RED TAPE. I PROBABLY SAVED ONLY ABOUT

$5,000 TO SOMETHING LESS THAN $6,000 WHEN EVERYTHING WAS COUNTED. COMPARING FLYING TO WASHINGTON STATE RATHER THAN DRIVING THERE.

YOU KNOW, I WAS SO IRRITATED BY THE THREE SKIPS THAT I THOUGHT ABOUT SENDING CANNED POTTED MEAT AND CRACKERS FOR THEM TO EAT. IT TOOK ME AWHILE TO ACT LIKE A DUCK AND LET IT ROLL OFF MY BACK. EVEN THEN EACH DROP OF WATER MUST HAVE MADE A BIG SPLASH WHEN IT HIT THE GROUND OR MAYBE WHEN IT HIT THE FAN. THINK ABOUT IT. BUT I GUESS IT WAS A GOOD THING TO TREAT THEM THE WAY I WANTED TO BE TREATED.

AFTER I BROUGHT THESE THREE SKIPS BACK TO VIRGINIA, THEY STAYED IN JAIL A FEW WEEKS AND THEIR ATTORNEY WAS ABLE TO GET THEM A BOND HEARING. AND THE SAME JUDGE, WHO GAVE ME ONLY THIRTY DAYS TO FIND THEM OR PAY A FORFEITURE FOR THE BOND, RELEASED THEM ON A P R BOND WHICH ALLOWED THEM TO GET OUT OF JAIL ON THEIR PROMISE TO APPEAR IN COURT.

WELL, WELL THERE'S MORE TO THIS STORY THAT MAKES ME LAUGH EVERY TIME I THINK ABOUT IT.

THESE THREE CHARACTERS DIDN'T SHOW FOR THEIR COURT APPEARANCE AGAIN AND GUESS WHERE THEY WENT. YOU GOT IT BACK TO WASHINGTON STATE. AND THIS TIME THE SHERIFF'S OFFICE HAD TO GO GET THEM. I WAS TOLD AFTER THE DEPUTIES WERE PAID, HOTEL ROOMS, MEALS, FLYING THREE PEOPLE TO WASHINGTON STATE AND SIX PEOPLE BACK AND OTHER EXPENSES THE COST WAS OVER TWELVE THOUSAND DOLLARS TO GET THEM BACK TO VIRGINIA.

THE REGULAR PRESIDING JUDGE WAS THERE FOR THEIR ARRAIGNMENT THIS TIME AND THEIR TRIAL AND THEY WERE IN JAIL FOR ALL THESE APPEARANCES BECAUSE THE JUDGE WASN'T TAKING ANY CHANCES FOR THEM TO TAKE FLIGHT (LITERALLY). AND EACH OF THEM RECEIVED PRISON TIME TO SERVE.

BUT YOU CAN BE ASSURED'

THIS AIN'T NO DOG.

As I think, which is hard for me to do. It hurts my head. Lol.

One cold and rainy night I received a call about a $10,000 bond. All THE INFORMATION about the bond sounded good. The person had never been in jail in the past and he had ties to the community. So, I told the caller I would meet her at the jail in 30 minutes. And I jumped in my vehicle and proceeded toward the jail. It usually took me about 20 to 30 minutes to get to this jail.

I was about HALFWAY to the jail when I saw what appeared to be an older woman trying to change a tire. And as I went past HER, something told me I had to go back and help her. Another thought was the $10,000 bond waiting on me. And I knew there were bondsmen around this jail most of the time. These bondsmen would take your bond from you if you were only a few minutes late. They would tell the ones wanting to do the bond that you wasn't coming and they would do the bond for them. You would lose your bond to these varmints if you wasn't Johnny on the spot.

But losing a thousand dollars didn't matter to me at that time, because I saw a picture in my mind, of this being Millie, my sister, my mother or any of the very important females in my life in the cold blowing rain trying to change a flat tire. And I could also imagine what if this woman was crippled or sick.

Well, that's all it took for me to turn my vehicle around and head back to help this woman. And as I approached the disabled vehicle, I could see she was an elderly woman possibly in her 70s. It was pouring a cold wind driven rain and in her vehicle was three children and a middle aged woman with a cast on her leg. She said they were her grandchildren and daughter who she had gone to their house to get them because their electricity had been turned off when her daughter

COULDN'T PAY THE BILL. SHE SAID HER DAUGHTER HAD A BAD MENTAL PROBLEM AND COULDN'T WORK.

I TOLD THE OLDER WOMAN TO GET IN HER VEHICLE AND TURN THE HEAT ON TO DRY OFF BEFORE SHE CAUGHT PNEUMONIA. SHE ENTERED HER VEHICLE AS I STARTED CHANGING THE TIRE. THE EXTRA TIRE SHE HAD LOOKED PRETTY THREAD BEAR AND I KNEW IT WOULDN'T GO VERY MANY MILES UNTIL IT WOULD GO FLAT, AND MY EXTRA TIRE WAS TOO BIG TO FIT HER CAR. AFTER I CHANGED THE TIRE AND PUT HER TOOLS BACK IN THE TRUNK, I APPROACHED THE OLDER WOMAN'S SIDE OF THE VEHICLE AND SHE ROLLED HER GLASS DOWN. I TOLD HER I HAD FINISHED CHANGING HER TIRE AND THAT HER SPAR WAS IN POOR CONDITION AND SHE NEEDED TO GET NEW TIRES ON HER VEHICLE AS SOON AS POSSIBLE. SHE SAID SHE WAS AFRAID OF THAT AND SHE GUESSED SHE WOULD JUST HAVE TO PRAY THAT THEY LASTED UNTIL SHE WAS ABLE TO GET TIRES. SHE SAID HER HUSBAND HAD PASSED AWAY NOT LONG AGO AND SHE WAS TRYING TO HELP HER DAUGHTER WHO HAD A NO GOOD HUSBAND WHO WOULDN'T WORK OR TRY TO HELP THE DAUGHTER OR GRANDCHILDREN.

THE OLDER WOMAN THANKED ME AND TOLD ME IF THERE WAS ANY WORK, SHE COULD DO TO PAY ME SHE WOULD TRY TO DO IT. I TOLD HER SHE DIDN'T OWE ME NOTHING AND I WAS GLAD I COULD HELP HER AND THE CHILDREN. SHE SAID SHE HAD TO STOP AT THE STORE AND GET SOMETHING FOR HER GRANDCHILDREN TO TAKE FOR THE FLU AND THAT THEY WERE ALL SICK. SAID THE HOSPITAL TOLD THEM THEY OWED TO MUCH MONEY AND THEY COULDN'T COME THERE FOR TREATMENT. THIS WAS AT A TIME WHEN THE HOSPITALS COULD GET BY WITH THAT. THANK GOD THINGS HAVE CHANGED TODAY AND NO HOSPITAL CAN TURN YOU AWAY. I TOLD HER I DIDN'T HAVE ANY WORK FOR HER TO DO AND THAT I WAS THANKFUL TO BE ABLE TO HELP HER AND THE CHILDREN, AND NOT TO WORRY ABOUT PAYING ME FOR IT BECAUSE I DIDN'T WANT ANYTHING FOR WHAT LITTLE I HAD DONE.

I ASKED HER WHERE SHE LIVED AND IF IT WAS O K WITH HER, I WOULD FOLLOW HER HOME TO MAKE SURE SHE GOT THERE O K. SHE TOLD ME AND THANKED ME AGAIN. AND AS I FOLLOWED HER, I COULD JUST SEE MY CHILDREN OR

GRANDCHILDREN BEING SICK AND THEIR GRANDMOTHER TRYING TO TAKE CARE OF THEM WHEN SHE COULD BARELY TAKE CARE OF HERSELF.

So, I FOLLOWED THEM HOME TO MAKE SURE THEY WERE O K. AND LIKE THE BIG OLD SOFTY THAT I AM I MUST HAVE HAD TEARS IN MY EYES WHEN WE ARRIVED, BECAUSE THINKING ABOUT THIS MADE ME FEEL SORRY FOR GRANNY AND THE CHILDREN AND I KNEW WHEN WE ARRIVED AT HER HOUSE, I WAS GOING TO GIVE HER MONEY FOR NEW TIRES AND MAKE SURE THEY HAD A WARM HOME WITH FOOD ENOUGH FOR THEM. I WENT INSIDE WITH HER WHEN SHE STOPPED AT A STORE AND GOT SOME COUGH SYRUP AND BABY ASPIRIN FOR THE CHILDREN AND I COULD SEE SHE DIDN'T HAVE EVEN A DOLLAR LEFT AFTER PAYING THE CLERK. I DELIBERATELY DROPPED A TWENTY DOLLAR BILL BEHIND HER, AND WHEN SHE TURNED TO LEAVE THE STORE, I SAID YOU DROPPED SOMETHING, AND I PICKED UP THE MONEY AND HANDED IT TO HER. SHE SAID THIS ISN'T MINE, SOMEONE ELSE MUST HAVE LOST IT. I SAID IT'S NOT MINE STICK IT IN YOUR POCKET, AND SHE FINALLY AGREED TO DO SO. GRANNY TOLD THE CLERK IF ANYONE ASKED ABOUT LOSING TWENTY DOLLARS TO LET HER KNOW AND SHE WOULD GIVE IT TO THEM. I TOLD HER NOT TO WORRY ABOUT IT, AND THE LORD WOULD PROVIDE. SHE SMILED IN A MANNER OF SAYING I KNOW THIS WAS YOUR MONEY.

WHEN WE GOT TO HER HOUSE I GOT OUT OF MY VEHICLE AND ASK IF I COULD CARRY THE LITTLE ONE INTO THE HOUSE SINCE SHE WAS ASLEEP. I ASK HOW OLD THE LITTLE GIRL WAS BECAUSE TO ME SHE WAS SO TINY I FIGURED SHE WAS 2 OR 3. THE GRANNY SAID SHE WAS 7 YEARS OLD AND THIS MADE ME WONDER WHY SHE WAS SO SMALL. WHEN I ASKED ABOUT HER BEING SO SMALL GRANNY SAID SHE HAD BEEN SICK SINCE SHE WAS BORN. THE LITTLE GIRL HUGGED ME WHEN I WAS LEAVING AND SHE WHISPERED IN MY EAR WILL YOU BE MY DADDY, BECAUSE MY DADDY DON'T LOVE US. I KISSED HER ON THE FOREHEAD WHILE I WAS TRYING TO KEEP THE TEARS OUT OF MY EYES SO I COULD SEE. I WHISPERED BACK TO HER YES, I'LL BE YOUR DADDY AND I LOVE YOU A BUNCH. I TOLD HER I WOULD SEE HER AGAIN IN A FEW DAYS. SHE SAID DO YOU PROMISE. I TOLD HER I WOULD BE BACK AND I PROMISED.

HERE I AM SEEING WITH MY OWN EYES THE NEED GRANNY AND THESE CHILDREN HAD FOR MONEY TO BUY EVEN THE ESSENTIALS. I TOLD GRANNY I WOULD MAKE A DEAL WITH HER IF SHE WOULD TAKE ME UP ON IT. SHE SAID SURE I WILL WHAT IS THE DEAL, AND SHE SAID SHE WOULD DO ANY WORK TO PAY ME FOR MY HELP. I TOLD HER I NEEDED SOMEONE TO HELP MILLIE IN THE OFFICE. SHE SAID I'LL DO ANY KIND OF WORK TO PAY YOU FOR YOUR KINDNESS.

SHE SAID SHE NEEDED A JOB BECAUSE HER HUSBAND HAD ONLY RECEIVED $450 PER MONTH FOR THEIR SOCIAL SECURITY RETIREMENT AND HE HAD DIED A FEW WEEKS AGO AND SHE HAD TO PAY THE LAST MONTH'S CHECK ON HIS FUNERAL EXPENSES SO HE WOULD BE BURIED. SHE SAID I'M NOT A BEGGAR BECAUSE I'LL WORK FOR ANY MONEY I CAN GET. AT THAT TIME, I REACHED IN MY POCKET AND GOT WHAT MONEY I HAD AND GIVE IT TO HER. THERE WAS PROBABLY A THOUSAND DOLLARS FROM WHERE I HAD DONE BONDS. I NEVER COUNTED IT BECAUSE IF IT HAD BEEN $50,000 IT WOULDN'T HAVE MATTERED BECAUSE I HAD TO HELP THIS FAMILY. SHE DIDN'T WANT TO TAKE THE MONEY AND I MADE HER TAKE IT.

I TOLD HER TO BUY WHATEVER SHE NEEDED FOR HER AND THE CHILDREN AND PAY FOR OTHER THINGS SHE NEEDED. GRANNY GOT TIRES FOR HER CAR AND PAID A LOT OF BILLS SO HER AND THE CHILDREN COULD CONTINUE TO LIVE IN THE HOUSE, AND ALL WINTER I WOULD STOP TO SEE THIS GRANNY AND THE CHILDREN TO MAKE SURE THEY WERE O K. I WOULD ALWAYS TAKE THE CHILDREN SOME CANDY, TOYS, AND STUFF. THE LITTLE GIRL WOULD RUN TO ME AND ALMOST JUMP AROUND MY NECK TO GIVE ME A HUG, AND SHE MUST HAVE TOLD ME A THOUSAND TIMES I LOVE YOU DADDY. WELL, THIS ALWAYS MADE ME CRY AND SOMETIMES SHE WOULD SAY ARE YOU CRYING, AND I WOULD SAY NO MY SINUSES ARE ACTING UP OR I HAVE AN ALLERGY. SHE WOULD TAKE HER TINY HAND AND WIPE MY FOREHEAD AND SAY IS IT BETTER NOW. I WOULD ALWAYS SAY YES. I WOULD TELL HER I WAS GIVING HER A BEAR HUG AND SHE WOULD SMILE AS I HUGGED HER. ONE DAY AS I TOLD HER I WAS GIVING HER A BEAR HUG SHE SAID YOU DON'T LOOK LIKE A BEAR, YOU'RE MY DADDY AND THAT MADE MY DAY.

AND EACH TIME I STOPPED GRANNY WOULD SAY WHEN DO YOU WANT ME TO START WORKING TO PAY YOU FOR WHAT YOU HAVE DONE FOR US. I WOULD ALWAYS SAY I'LL LET YOU KNOW. I KNEW I WOULD NEVER ASK HER TO DO ANY WORK BECAUSE SHE COULD BARELY GET AROUND LET ALONE DO ANY WORK. BESIDES THAT, SHE HAD HER CHILDREN THERE WITH HER.

I ASKED IF HER AND THE CHILDREN HAD FOOD AND SHE SAID THEY HAD ENOUGH AND THAT SHE HAD RAISED A GARDEN AND HAD CANNED MUCH OF IT. SHE ALSO SAID YOU HAVE DONE TOO MUCH FOR US AND WE CAN NEVER THANK YOU ENOUGH.

THE SAME NIGHT I HELPED GRANNY I PROCEEDED ON TO THE JAIL AND AS I SUSPECTED ANOTHER BONDSMAN HAD DONE MY $10,000 BOND, BUT THAT DIDN'T MATTER I HAD RECEIVED WHAT MONEY COULDN'T BUY AND THAT WAS A GOOD FEELING FROM HELPING SOMEONE IN NEED.

I NEVER WENT WRONG IN HELPING PEOPLE WHO REALLY NEEDED HELP. THE LORD WILL ALWAYS BLESS YOU TEN TIMES FOLD WHEN YOU EXTEND A HELPING HAND TO THOSE IN NEED.

AND AS BAD THINGS HAPPENING WOULD HAVE IT, I BEGAN TO GET SICK ONE NIGHT AND HAD TO BE TAKEN TO THE HOSPITAL. THEY KEPT ME THERE FOR ABOUT TWO WEEKS BEFORE I BEGAN TO FEEL BETTER. I WAS TERRIBLY SICK. IT SURELY MUST HAVE BEEN A POWERFUL STRAIN OF FLU. AND EVEN AFTER I WAS TAKEN HOME IT TOOK A FEW MORE DAYS BEFORE I COULD DRIVE.

AND AS I GOT STRONG ENOUGH, I DROVE TO GRANNY'S HOUSE ONLY TO FIND IT EMPTY WITH NO SIGHT OF GRANNY OR THE CHILDREN. I HURRIED TO A NEIGHBOR'S HOUSE AND ASK A FELLOW STANDING OUTSIDE WHERE THE OLDER LADY AND THE CHILDREN WERE THAT HAD LIVED IN THE HOUSE. HE SAID ALL HE KNEW WAS THE OLD LADY AND CHILDREN HAD MOVED SOMEWHERE IN TENNESSEE. HE SAID SOMEONE TOLD HIM THE WELFARE PEOPLE WERE GOING TO TAKE THE CHILDREN FROM THE OLD WOMAN AFTER HER DAUGHTER WENT OFF HER ROCKER AND LEFT THEM. THE OLD GENT SAID SHE HAD GONE TO LIVE WITH ONE OF HER FRIENDS

SOMEWHERE IN TENNESSEE. THIS NEWS MADE ME CRY AND SMILE AT THE SAME TIME. I KNEW THAT IF THERE WAS ANY WAY GRANNY COULD TAKE CARE OF THOSE CHILDREN SHE WOULD. I STILL MISS THE LITTLE HAND OF THE TINY GIRL PUSHING MY HAIR BACK TO KISS ME ON THE FOREHEAD AND SAYING IS IT BETTER NOW DADDY. AND WITH A SAD HEART I THINK ABOUT THEM. SO, I HAVE SAID MANY PRAYERS FOR THIS FAMILY AND VERY MUCH ADMIRE THE STRENGTH GRANNY FOUND TO TAKE CARE OF HER GRANDCHILDREN. I KNOW IF THERE IS A HEAVEN THIS FAMILY WILL BE THERE. AND EACH TIME I GO BY THE HOUSE GRANNY AND HER LITTLE GRANDCHILDREN HAD LIVED I GET CHOKED UP BUT ALWAYS KNOW THEY ARE VERY WELL TAKEN CARE OF. YOU CAN NEVER GO WRONG WITH A GRANNY'S LOVE.

MY HILLBILLYONTICS TRAINING HAS SERVED ME WELL IN HOW TO HELP OTHERS.

AND YOU PROBABLY KNOW BY NOW.

THIS AIN'T NO DOG.

AS ALWAYS IT SEEMS AS THOUGH MY LIFE HAS CONSISTED OF WORKING OR RESTING. AND ONE EVENING WHILE I WAS RESTING AND EATING SUPPER A FRIEND OF MINE WHO WAS A JUDGE CALLED ME AND ASKED IF I WOULD DO A BOND FOR HIM. AND WHILE KNOWING THIS GENTLEMAN FOR QUITE A WHILE, I KNEW HE WAS A GOOD MAN WHO HAD WENT OUT OF HIS WAY TO HELP FOLKS IN EVERY WAY. AND THIS WAS NO EXCEPTION. I TOLD HIM I SURE WOULD AND ASK WHO THE BOND WAS FOR. HE TOLD ME THE FELLOW'S NAME AND WE SET A TIME TO MEET AT THE JAIL TO DO THE BOND.

OVER THE YEARS THIS JUDGE HAD DONE BONDS FOR PEOPLE TO HELP THEM GET OUT OF JAIL WHILE WAITING ON THEIR TRIAL. THIS MAN TRULY BELIEVES IN A PERSON BEING INNOCENT UNTIL PROVEN GUILTY. AND THAT EVERYONE HAD A RIGHT TO A FAIR TRIAL.

WHEN I ARRIVED AT THE JAIL MY JUDGE FRIEND WAS ALREADY THERE WAITING. I HAD MILLIE WITH ME SO, HE AND HIS WIFE GOT IN THE BACK SEAT TO GIVE ME THE INFORMATION ON THE ONE HE WAS BONDING.

HE AND HIS WIFE BOTH WERE VERY FRIENDLY FOLKS WHO I AM PROUD TO SAY THEY ARE MY FRIENDS. THE JUDGE AND HIS WIFE ALSO DID A LOT OF MISSIONARY WORK WHILE HELPING PEOPLE OF ALL WALKS OF LIFE. THEY SPENT A LOT OF TIME AND MONEY HELPING PEOPLE HAVE A BETTER LIFE. THEY PROVIDED FOOD, CLOTHING, A PLACE TO LIVE, JOBS AND ALL THE ESSENTIAL THINGS NEEDED TO LIVE. THESE FOLKS WERE VERY MUCH GOD'S ANGELS WHILE THEY WENT A MILLION MILES OUT OF THEIR WAY TO HELP MANKIND AND GUILD THEM IN THE RIGHT DIRECTION. I HAVE WATCHED THE JUDGE IN HIS COURTROOM WHILE HE WOULD HELP PROVIDE WORK PROGRAMS, DRUG AND ALCOHOL ABUSE PROGRAMS AND OTHER ASSISTANCE TO DEFENDANTS IN NEED. NO ONE COULD HAVE BEEN ANY FAIRER TO THESE PEOPLE. AND FROM THE BOTTOM OF THEIR HEART'S, THEY PULLED EVERYTHING OUT TO SHARE AND HELP.

IT TOOK A WHILE TO FILL OUT THE FORMS TO BOND THE DEFENDANT. ALSO, I GUESS WE NEEDED TO SHARE WITH EACH OTHER ALL THE GOOD THINGS THE PEOPLE HE AND HIS WIFE HAD SEEN OUT OF THE PEOPLE THEY HAD HELPED. I WAS ALWAYS GLAD TO SEE THESE FOLKS BECAUSE OF THE KINDNESS AND GOODNESS THEY HAVE SHARED.

AFTER I FILLED OUT ALL THE NECESSARY FORMS CONCERNING THE DEFENDANT AND THE JUDGE AND HIS WIFE PAID FOR THE BOND OUT OF THEIR OWN POCKET AND SIGNED TO ASSURE THE DEFENDANT WOULD SHOW FOR COURT, I PROCEEDED INTO THE JAIL AND THE MAGISTRATE'S OFFICE TO DO THE BOND ON THE DEFENDANT.

IT TOOK A WHILE FOR THE JAILORS TO DO THEIR PAPERWORK AND RELEASE FORMS SO THE DEFENDANT COULD BE LET OUT OF JAIL. SO, THE JUDGE AND HIS WIFE AND MILLIE AND MYSELF HAD TIME TO TALK WHILE ENJOYING EACH OTHER'S COMPANY.

FINALLY, WHEN THE DEFENDANT WAS RELEASED AND CAME OVER TO MY VEHICLE TO SIGN MY PAPERWORK, I TOLD HIM THAT HE BETTER APPRECIATE THE JUDGE AND HIS WIFE FOR HELPING HIM. I TOLD HIM HOW THE JUDGE AND HIS WIFE HAD PAID FOR THE BOND WITH THEIR MONEY AND SINGED TO ASSURE THEM THAT HE

SHOWED FOR COURT. I SAID AND YOU BETTER NOT LET THEM DOWN AND IF THEY EVER NEED YOUR HELP, YOU BETTER BE THERE FOR THEM.

I SHOOK HANDS WITH THIS VERY HONORABLE JUDGE AND TOLD HIM IF HE GOT A CHANCE TO COME BY OUR HOME AND VISIT ANY TIME. I CAN HONESTLY SAY I HAVE NEVER SEEN A MORE HELPFUL PERSON TO PEOPLE IN NEED THAN THIS JUDGE AND HIS WIFE.

THAT GOES TO SHOW YOU THAT AMONGST JUDGES AND PEOPLE IN THE CRIMINAL JUSTICE FIELD THERE ARE THOSE WHO HAVE A HEART AND CARE ABOUT PEOPLE.

AND AS I ALWAYS SAY"

THIS AIN'T NO DOG.

ONE NIGHT WHILE DOING A BOND AT A JAIL IN ANOTHER COUNTY, I WAS APPROACHED BY THIS OLDER LADY WHO ASKED ARE YOU A BONDSMAN. I RESPONDED YES MAM CAN I HELP YOU. SHE SAID YES, MY SON IS IN JAIL HERE AND I WANT TO BOND HIM OUT. I ASKED WHAT HE WAS CHARGED WITH AND SHE STATED DISTURBING THE PEACE AND ASSAULT. I ASKED HOW MUCH THE BOND WAS, WHERE HE LIVED AND ALL THE PERTINENT INFORMATION NEEDED BEFORE I AGREED TO DO THE BOND. EVERYTHING SEEMED TO BE O K SO I TOLD HER I WOULD DO THE BOND AND THE COST WOULD BE $500 FOR THE $5,000 BOND. SHE SAID SHE COULD PAY FOR THE BOND IF I WOULD DO IT. SO, I TOLD HER I WOULD, AND BEGAN TO DO THE PAPERWORK.

AFTER I DID THE PAPERWORK, I TOLD THE JAILORS ON DUTY I WAS READY TO GO BEFORE THE MAGISTRATE TO DO THE BOND. ONE OF THE JAILORS TOSSED ME THE KEY TO THE MAGISTRATES OFFICE AND SAID I'LL BRING HIM DOWN FROM THE UPSTAIRS PART OF THE JAIL. AS ONE OF THE JAILORS OPENED THE MAIN DOOR LEADING INTO THE JAIL CELLS THE OTHER PROCEEDED UPSTAIRS INSIDE THE JAIL TO GET THE BOY I WAS GOING TO BOND. THE BOY'S MOTHER WAS WAITING IN A ROOM OFF TO THE SIDE OF THE MAIN ENTRANCE OF THE JAIL BUILDING.

Soon the jailor came downstairs with the boy and said Clyde, he's ready to go. And bring us back the paperwork you get from the magistrate. I told him I would as I went out of the main entrance and toward the magistrate's office. The boy I was bonding followed behind me until we reached a building the magistrate was located in. He was a stocky built fellow who looked like he could wrestle bears. I unlocked the main door and motioned for the boy to come on. He proceeded in the door behind me and we proceeded down a hall until we arrived AT a white door that had a sign on it that said knock before entering. As I knocked on the door a voice from inside the door said come in. I opened the door and pointed to the inside of the door and the boy I was bonding proceeded inside. A small like man with gray hair and glasses was standing behind an old wooden desk with two old wooden chairs in front of the desk. The old magistrate said sit down boys and rest a spell and what can I do for you gentlemen. I told him I needed to do a bond for the boy with me. I reached him the papers I brought from the jail and the magistrate said all right I'll see what I can do for you boys and he got some papers out of a bin behind him while starting to write. I liked this old gent because he was so kind and took such an interest in his work as to make sure everything was done right.

After a short while he asked the FELLOW, I was bonding to sign some forms he had filled out, and after doing so he ask him to raise his right hand and if he swore that the INFORMATION, he give was the truth the whole truth and nothing but the truth. The fellow told the magistrate I do. And as the magistrate handed the fellow a copy of the paper's he said what else can I do for y'all today. I told him that was all today. He told me well you come sit and talk with me sometime when you can. I told him I would and thanked him as we went out the door.

This Ain't no dog.

I TOOK THE PAPERS I RECEIVED FROM THE MAGISTRATE AND GIVE ONE COPY TO THE JAILORS AS I KEPT A COPY FOR MY RECORDS. I THANKED THE JAILORS FOR THEIR HELP AND TOLD THEM I WOULD SEE THEM LATER. BOTH JAILORS TOLD ME IT WAS GOOD TO SEE ME AND TO HURRY BACK AND TAKE SOME MORE OFF THEIR HANDS. THEY EACH LAUGHED ONE WITH A VERY LOUD SOUND. IT MADE ME LAUGH TO HEAR HIM LAUGH. I TOLD THEM I WOULD AND PROCEEDED TO MY VEHICLE AND HEADED FOR HOME. I HAD BEEN GONE FOR ABOUT 10 HOURS AND BEGIN TO GET TIRED.

UNFORTUNATELY, ABOUT TWO MONTHS LATER I HAD A DEPUTY TO BRING ME A SHOWCAUSE. I HAD TO GO TO COURT AND TELL THE JUDGE WHERE THE DEFENDANT WAS AND OR WHAT I KNEW ABOUT HIM.

I KNEW I HAD TO FIND THIS BOY AND PUT HIM BACK IN JAIL OR PAY A FORFEITURE FOR HIS BOND. SO, I WENT FROM SLOW GEAR TO HIGH GEAR IN LOCATING HIM. I CALLED HIS MOTHER WHO HAD BONDED HIM OUT AND TOLD HER WHAT WAS GOING ON. I ASKED HER IF SHE KNEW WHERE HE WAS, AND SHE SAID HE WAS STAYING IN AN OLD HOUSE ON THE HILL ABOVE HER HOUSE. SHE SAID IF YOU GO AFTER HIM TO BE CAREFUL BECAUSE HE IS DRINKING AND HAS AN OLD 12 GAUGE SHOTGUN. AND THERE'S NOTHING WORSE THAN A 12 GAUGE SHOTGUN THAN AN OLD 12 GAUGE SHOTGUN. THE SPRINGS AND OTHER PARTS IN OLD GUNS MAKE THEM MORE DANGEROUS BECAUSE THEY DISCHARGE EASIER AND QUICKER THAN NEWER GUNS.

SO HERE I AM GOING DOWN THE ROAD TO TRY TO APPREHEND A BAIL SKIP BY MYSELF. AND KNOWING THAT THE BAIL SKIP IS DRINKING AND WHALING AN OLD 12 GAUGE SHOTGUN. YOU KNOW THE LORD MADE ME SANE WHEN I WAS BORN AND I DON'T KNOW WHAT HAPPENED OVER THE YEARS.

AFTER TRAVELING ABOUT 30 MILES TOWARD WHERE THE BAIL SKIP WAS LOCATED, I BEGAN TO THINK ABOUT MY SIG SAUER I WAS PACKING. I FELT FOR THE EXTRA 9 MM MAGAZINES IN MY FIREARMS BAG AND THERE WERE NONE. I HAD TAUGHT A FIREARM'S CLASS THE DAY BEFORE AND HADN'T REPLACED MY 9MM MAGAZINES

IN MY FIREARMS BAG, BUT THAT WAS O K BECAUSE THE MAGAZINE IN MY SIG WAS LOADED WITH 15 ROUNDS. AND, THEN I BEGAN TO THINK ABOUT THE FIREARMS CLASS I TAUGHT WHERE I ALWAYS MADE SURE MY FIREARMS WERE EMPTY BEFORE DEMONSTRATING THEM IN THE CLASSROOM. I IMMEDIATELY DREW MY SIG OUT OF ITS HOLSTER AND DROPPED THE MAGAZINE. OH, SHIT THE MAGAZINE WAS EMPTY. AND I BEGAN TO THINK FAST BECAUSE WITHIN 10 OR 12 MILES I WOULD BE WHERE THE BAIL SKIP WAS. I THOUGHT YEAH THAT'S WHAT I'LL DO, I FAKE IT. I'LL PRETEND AS IF MY SIG IS LOADED.

AS I APPROACHED THE MOTHER'S HOUSE, SHE WAS STANDING IN THE YARD AND FLAGGED ME DOWN. SHE SAID HE HAS A SHOTGUN AND IS DRINKING MOONSHINE. SHE SAID HE WILL SHOOT YOU IF YOU ARE NOT CAREFUL. AND I THOUGHT OH SHIT AS I STARTED DRIVING UP THE HILL TO THE OLD HOUSE WHERE THE BAIL SKIP WAS. FEAR DIDN'T STOP ME FROM BECOMING A BAIL BONDSMAN SO IT WASN'T GOING TO STOP ME NOW. LIKE RIDING A ROLLER COASTER, HANG ONTO YOUR HAT.

I PARKED MY VEHICLE ABOUT 100 YARDS BEFORE I REACHED THE HOUSE. I OPENED MY DOOR AS QUIETLY AS I COULD AND SILENTLY SLIPPED FROM THE DRIVER'S SEAT ONTO THE DIRT DRIVEWAY. I CROUCHED AS I MADE MY WAY TO THE OLD HOUSE. I FELT VERY UNCOMFORTABLE CARRYING AN EMPTY GUN WHILE KNOWING THE BAIL SKIP HAD A LOADED 12 GAUGE SHOTGUN. WHEN I REACHED THE PORCH OF THE OLD HOUSE I PRAYED TWO PRAYERS, ONE WAS THAT THE BOARDS ON THE OLD PORCH DIDN'T CREAK AND THE OTHER WAS THAT I DIDN'T GET SHOT WHILE TRYING TO APPREHEND THE BAIL SKIP. I HAD A LOT OF OTHER PRAYERS TO SAY BUT I DIDN'T HAVE TIME TO GET ALL OF THEM IN AT THAT TIME.

I CROUCHED AS LOW AS I COULD WHILE ATTEMPTING TO INCH MY WAY ACROSS THE PORCH. AND OLD LORD THE BOARDS STARTED CREAKING. I THOUGHT THE LORD TOOK CARE OF THAT FOR ME, BUT I GUESS HE COULDN'T DO EVERYTHING. SO, I KEPT GOING WHILE MY SENSE OF SMARTS SAID RUN AND MY SENSE OF STUPIDITY SAID WE'RE GOING TO GET THIS BAIL SKIP. AND AS I NEARED THE DOOR, I REALIZED I DIDN'T HAVE A PLAN. I THOUGHT WHAT PLAN WOULD HAVE WORKED? OH WELL TOO LATE NOW SAYS ME. I DIDN'T HAVE A CLUE, BUT I WOULD PLAY IT BY EAR.

I SLOWLY AND SILENTLY REACHED FOR THE DOORKNOB AND LIKE A PROTECTIVE HOMEOWNER WOULD DO, IT WAS LOCKED. WHAT NOW SHERLOCK? I COULD TRY TO BREAK IT DOWN WITH MY SHOULDER, AND THEN I FELT THE PAIN FIRST FROM HITTING THE DOOR WITH MY SHOULDER AND SECOND FROM THE BLAST OF THE 12 GAUGE SHOTGUN SENDING ME TO THE PROMISED LAND BEFORE I WAS READY TO GO. NO GOOD IN THAT THOUGHT. SO THERE LET'S LEAVE. NOT SO FAST SAID MY STUPID SIDE OF ME. WE ARE GOING TO CATCH US A BAIL SKIP. BUT HOW SAID THE SMART SIDE? I GUESS WE SHOULD KNOCK ON THE DOOR AND SEE IF ANYONE IS HOME, AND I KEPT HEARING THE SHOTGUN BLAST AS IT KILLED BOTH OF ME, MY SMART SIDE AND MY DUMBASS SIDE. BUT AS ONLY MORE FEAR COULD HOLD ME BACK, I KNOCKED ON THE DOOR. SMART SIDE WISHED NO ONE WAS HOME WHILE THE DUMBASS SIDE SAID BRING IT ON. AND IN JUST A FLASH THE DOOR FLEW OPEN AND THERE STOOD THE BAIL SKIP WITH THE OLD 12 GAUGE POINTED STRAIGHT AT ME. I KNEW I DIDN'T HAVE MUCH CHARM, BUT WHAT I HAD I BETTER USE IT NOW.

I SAID HOW ARE YOU DOING WHILE TRYING TO IGNORE THE SHOTGUN. WITH A SLURRED VOICE HE SAID A HELL OF A LOT BETTER THAN YOU BECAUSE I GOT THE SHOTGUN LOADED FOR BEAR AND YOU DON'T HAVE YOUR GUN OUT OF ITS HOLSTER. I EASED MY HAND DOWN AND TOOK HOLD OF MY SIG AND GENTLY DREW IT OUT AND AIMED IT AT HIS BALLS AND SAID I COULD SHOOT YOUR BALLS OFF BEFORE YOU COULD SHOOT ME. HE LOOKED DOWN AND SAW MY SIG WAS REALLY AIMED AT HIS BALLS. HE DIDN'T KNOW THAT I HAD NO AMMUNITION AS HE STARTED TO STUTTER WHILE SAYING YOU WOULDN'T SHOOT A MAN IN THE BALLS WOULD YOU. HE SAID THAT WOULD RUIN A MAN FOR LIFE. MY DAD LOST HIS WHILE SLIDING OFF A SHARP ROCK AFTER I WAS BORN. AND I BEGIN TO SEE HE WAS AFRAID THAT I WOULD SHOOT HIM IN HIS BALLS.

AS I BEGAN TO FEEL REAL BRAVE, I TOLD HIM I WOULD MAKE A DEAL WITH HIM, IF HE WOULD PUT THE SHOTGUN DOWN REAL EASY LIKE, I WOULDN'T SHOOT HIM THERE. I KNEW IF HE BUMPED THE SHOTGUN AGAINST SOMETHING IT COULD GO OFF AND INJURE OR KILL ME OR HIM OR BOTH. SO, I HAD TO KEEP CONVINCING HIM THAT IF I SHOT HIM IN HIS BALLS, IT WOULD HURT SOMETHING AWFUL AND EVEN RUIN HIS MANHOOD FOREVER.

I MUST HAVE SAID THE MAGIC WORDS, BECAUSE IN A SHORT WHILE HE LOWERED THE SHOTGUN JUST ENOUGH THAT I COULD GRAB IT AND FORCE IT OUT OF HIS HANDS. AND THEN THE FIGHT WAS ON. HE SWUNG AT ME WITH HIS LEFT HAND AND HIT THE OLD SHOTGUN AND IT WAS COCKED AND WENT OFF SENDING THE SHOT THROUGH THE ROOF. I WAS JUST GLAD I WASN'T BETWEEN THE SHOTGUN AND THE ROOF. AFTER THAT I THREW HIM TO THE FLOOR AS HARD AS I COULD. I KNEW I HAD TO BRING HIM UNDER CONTROL AND IN HANDCUFFS. I DROPPED THE SHOTGUN ON THE FLOOR AND LET MY SIG FALL ONTO THE FLOOR AS WELL. AS HE HIT THE FLOOR HIS HEAD BOUNCED UP AND DOWN LIKE A RUBBER BALL AND I JUMPED ON TOP OF HIM AND ROLLED HIM ONTO HIS STOMACH. I HAD TO ACT FAST BEFORE HE REGAINED HIS STABILITY. I REACHED INTO MY HOLSTER CASE AND RETRIEVED MY SMITH AND WESSON CUFFS. I PLACED HIS LEFT HAND IN A CUFF AND THEN HIS RIGHT HAND. I GRABBED MY ANKLE LEG IRONS AND QUICKLY PLACED AN ANKLE IN EACH ONE OF THE CUFFS. I LEARNED THE HARD WAY SOME PEOPLE CAN KICK LIKE A MULE WITH THEIR FEET WHEN NOT IN CUFFS.

I GAVE A SIGH OF RELIEF AND THANKED THE LORD I WAS STILL ALIVE. IT WILL BE OUR TIME TO GO SOON ENOUGH, BUT THE LORD SPARED ME ANOTHER DAY AND UNTIL ANOTHER TIME. I HAVE PLACED MYSELF IN HARM'S WAY AT TIMES WHEN I SHOULD HAVE NOT LISTENED TO MY SENSE OF STUPIDITY AND IT WOULD HAVE BEEN WISER AND SAFER TO LISTEN TO MY SENSE OF SMARTS. ALCOHOL AND FIREARMS NEVER MIX VERY WELL AND CAUSE PEOPLE TO DO SOME STUPID THINGS. I COULD HAVE CHARGED THE BAIL SKIP WITH ATTEMPTED MURDER AND OTHER THINGS, BUT I WAS ABLE TO GET HIM BACK TO THE JAIL SAFELY AND NO HARM WAS DONE. I JUST HOPE THE BAIL SKIP THINKS SERIOUSLY ABOUT HIS POTENTIALLY KILLING SOMEONE OR GETTING KILLED. IT WOULD MAKE HIM A SMARTER PERSON.

THIS AIN'T NO DOG,

BUT THERE WAS A SCARRED DOG AS I WENT ABOUT MY DUTIES AS A BAIL BONDSMAN.

ONCE UPON A TIME AS THE STORY BOOK GOES, I BONDED A BOY OUT OF JAIL, WHO TOLD ME HOW HARD HE COULD WORK, AND IF I NEEDED SOMEONE TO WORK, HE WOULD WORK FOR A VERY CHEAP WAGE. I TOLD HIM TO COME TO MY HOUSE A CERTAIN DAY AND TIME AND I WOULD TALK TO HIM.

THE I HAD TOLD THE BOY TO COME SEE ME ABOUT WORKING WAS AT A TIME I WAS OUTSIDE SHOVELING GRAVELS INTO A WHEELBARROW AND HAULING THEM ABOUT 150 YARDS TO A PLACE I WAS DUMPING THEM. I WAS ABOUT READY TO QUIT FOR THE DAY AS I STOPPED WORKING TO TALK TO THE BOY.

I TOLD HIM HE COULDN'T CHANGE HIS PAST, BUT HE COULD SURELY ALTER HIS FUTURE. I SAID I WILL GIVE YOU A CHANCE TO SHOW ME YOU ARE SERIOUS ABOUT WORKING AND WALKING THE STRAIGHT AND NARROW PATH OF DOING GOOD IN LIFE. I TOLD HIM IF I CAUGHT HIM INTO DRUGS OR ANY CRIMINAL ACTIONS THAT HIS CHANCE WITH ME WOULD BE OVER. I SAID I DON'T MIND HELPING YOU AND I WOULD LIKE TO SEE YOU DO GOOD BUT DON'T SCREW UP. HE SAID HE WAS SERIOUS AND HE WOULD SEE ME THE NEXT DAY AT 8 AM.

THE NEXT DAY HE SHOWED UP LIKE HE WAS SUPPOSED TO. HE WAS THERE AT 8 AM. I WAS HAULING GRAVELS IN WHEELBARROWS. I SHOWED HIM WHERE I WANTED THE GRAVEL HAULED TOO. IT WAS ABOUT 150 YARDS TO WHERE I WANTED THEM DUMPED. I HAD TWO WHEELBARROWS AND PLENTY OF DIFFERENT KINDS OF SHOVELS. AND I TOLD HIM TO PICK THE WHEELBARROW AND SHOVEL HE WANTED TO USE.

AS EXPECTED, HE PICKED THE EASIEST ROLLING WHEELBARROW AND A ROUND POINTED SHOVEL. I DIDN'T HAVE A PROBLEM WITH HIS CHOICE OF WHEELBARROW OR SHOVEL. I JUST WANTED TO SEE WHAT THIS YOUNG MAN WAS MADE OF AND HOW MUCH ENDURANCE HE HAD. WE STOPPED ABOUT EVERY HOUR AND DRANK GATOR AID TO KEEP US HYDRATED AS THE SUN HAD BECAME VERY HOT AND PULLED THE MOISTER OUT OF YOU.

WE WORKED UNTIL ABOUT 1 P M AND I ASKED HIM IF HE WAS HUNGRY AND HE REPLIED NO JUST THIRSTY AGAIN. I INSISTED THAT HE EAT A SANDWICH WITH ME

AS WE MADE OUR WAY TO MY HOUSE WHERE I MADE US SANDWICHES. HE ATE A FEW BITES FROM HIS AND SAID I NEVER EAT LUNCH BECAUSE IT MAKES ME LAZY. I TOLD HIM IT WOULD KEEP UP HIS STRENGTH SO HE COULD KEEP UP WITH THE OLD MAN. HE WAS IN HIS THIRTIES AND I WAS IN MY SIXTIES AT THAT TIME.

I BEGAN WORKING THIS YOUNG MAN AND TRYING TO HELP HIM GET RE-ESTABLISHED IN LIFE. I BEGAN TO LEARN THINGS THAT OCCURRED IN HIS LIFE AS WE WORKED ON SEVERAL PROJECTS THROUGHOUT THE COMING DAYS, I BEGAN TO TRUST HIM MORE AND MORE. I DID SO TO THE POINT I WOULD LEAVE HIM TO DO A JOB WE STARTED WHILE I PROCEEDED TO DO OTHER THINGS BUT MOSTLY TO THE JAILS TO DO BONDS OR SOME TYPE TRAINING FOR MY BAIL BONDS BUSINESS.

AS TIME WENT ON, HE LOST HIS PLACE WHERE HE WAS LIVING AND WAS HOMELESS. WHEN THIS OCCURRED, I LET HIM MOVE INTO A STUDIO APARTMENT I HAD AT MY HOUSE. I TOLD HIM AS LONG AS HE KEPT WALKING THE STRAIGHT AND NARROW, HE COULD LIVE IN THE APARTMENT FREE AND I WOULD PAY ALL HIS UTILITIES. HE CONTINUED TO WORK, AND WAS DEDICATED TO WORKING ON THE PROPERTIES WHILE LEARNING A TRADE, AS I WOULD TELL HIM IF HE WOULD PAY ATTENTION, HE COULD LEARN TO DO MANY CONSTRUCTION JOBS THAT WOULD HELP HIM IN HIS LIFE.

THIS AIN'T NO DOG.

FOR ABOUT FOUR YEARS THE YOUNG MAN DID A GOOD JOB WHILE WORKING ON MY PROPERTIES AND WAS LEARNING HOW TO DO MANY THINGS. I TRIED TO ENCOURAGE HIM TO LEARN ALL HE COULD SO HE COULD GET A GOOD JOB WORKING IN THE CONSTRUCTION FIELD. I FELT GOOD ABOUT MY EFFORTS WHILE HELPING SOMEONE CHANGE THEIR LIFE AROUND AND MAKE SOMETHING OUT OF THEMSELVES. I DEPENDED ON HIM TO THE POINT II COULD TELL HIM WHAT I NEEDED DONE AND HE WOULD DO THE JOB. I COULDN'T ASK FOR ANY BETTER HELPER THEN HE WAS.

BUT AS TIME WENT ON, I BEGAN TO SEE A CHANGE IN HIS ACTIONS AND HIS WANTING TO LEARN. HE BEGAN TO HAVE CONTACT WITH DIFFERENT PEOPLE WHO

I DID NOT KNOW. I TALKED TO HIM WHILE QUESTIONING WHO THESE PEOPLE WERE. HE TOLD ME THESE WERE SOME OLD FRIENDS HE KNEW FOR YEARS AND HE HAD WORKED WITH THEM.

I GUESS I WAS VULNERABLE TO HIS LIES THAT GOT WORSE AS TIME WENT ON. AND HIS RUDE ARBITRARY ACTIONS TOWARD ME GOT WORSE. AND ONE DAY HE ASKED ME IF A GIRL HE HAD MET COULD STAY WITH HIM A FEW DAYS. I TOLD HIM I WOULD HAVE TO TALK WITH HER TO SEE HOW SHE ACTED.

HE BROUGHT HER TO MY HOUSE ONE EVENING TO MEET ME AND I TALKED TO HER AS TO ATTEMPT TO LEARN HOW SHE ACTED. SHE KEPT RELATING TO KNOWING HIM A LONG TIME AND HOW SHE LOVED HIM SO MUCH. SHE GAVE ME THE PITCH OF HOW SHE WANTED TO GET A JOB AND MAKE BOTH THEIR LIVES SO MUCH BETTER SO THEY COULD GET MARRIED. SHE ALSO STATED SHE WAS HOMELESS BECAUSE HER MOTHER HAD DIED, AND HER FATHER WAS AN ALCOHOLIC WHILE ABUSING HER AND FINALLY FORCING HER TO LEAVE THE HOME. SHE SAID SHE HAD BEEN STAYING WITH FRIENDS AND SHE FELT LIKE SHE WAS IMPOSING ON THEM TOO MUCH. WELL, SHE GOT MY SYMPATHY AND I LET HER MOVE IN WITH HIM. WHICH WAS A MISTAKE ON MY PART AS I LATTER FOUND OUT.

IN A SHORT TIME, HE STARTED COMING OUT TO WORK WITH BLOOD SHOT EYES AND A SLURRED VOICE. I KNEW FROM SEEING OTHER PEOPLE THIS WAY THAT HE HAD TAKEN SOME KIND OF DRUG. I TOLD HIM TO GO BACK INTO HIS APARTMENT AND STRAIGHTEN UP AND NEVER TO COME TO WORK THAT WAY AGAIN.

THE NEXT DAY HE APOLOGIZED AND SAID IT WOULD NEVER HAPPEN AGAIN. I TOLD HIM I WOULDN'T TOLERATE THAT KIND OF BEHAVIOR AND IF IT HAPPENED AGAIN, HE COULD LEAVE MY PREMISES. AND AS TIME WENT ON FOR A WHILE HE ACTED O K AND WORKED DOING THINGS I NEEDED DONE.

ONE OCTOBER MORNING AS I WAS PREPARING TO WORK ON DIFFERENT THINGS AROUND MY HOUSE MY HELPER CAME OUT AND APPROACHED ME IN A STAGGERING MANNER AND I JUST ABOUT KNEW HE HAD TAKEN SOME TYPE OF DRUG. I ASK HIM WHAT HE HAD BEEN TAKING AND HE SAID NOT NOTHING WHILE

HE BEGAN TO CURSE AND GO INTO SOMEWHAT OF A RAGE. I TOLD HIM TO SHUT UP AND GO BACK INTO HIS APARTMENT AND GET HIS THINGS READY BECAUSE HE HAD TO LEAVE. HE SAID I'M NOT GOING ANYWHERE AND YOU CAN'T MAKE ME LEAVE BECAUSE YOU WILL HAVE TO GO TO COURT TO GET ME TO MOVE.

NO DOUBT HE HAD TALKED TO THE GIRL WHO HE HAD LIVING WITH HIM AND SHE HAD PLANTED IDEALS IN HIS HEAD. SHE HAD PLANTED MORE THAN IDEALS BECAUSE I WAS PRETTY SURE SHE HAD STARTED HIM TAKING DRUGS.

I HAD GIVEN HIM A CHANCE TO ACHIEVE IN LIFE AND MAKE SOMETHING OUT OF HIMSELF AND WHILE HE DID SOME STUPID THINGS THAT HIS GIRLFRIEND HAD PRESENTED TO HIM AND HE FOLLOWED HER LEAD. AND I TOLD HIM AGAIN HE HAD TO LEAVE. HE SAID I WANT LEAVE UNTIL THE COURTS MAKE ME.

I KNEW THAT I WOULD HAVE TO GO THROUGH ALL THE LEGAL CHANNELS TO FORCE HIM TO MOVE OUT OF MY APARTMENT. TO HAVE TO FORCE HIM OUT OF MY APARTMENT AND OFF MY PROPERTY BECAUSE OF HIS CHOICE TO FALL BACK INTO THE DRUG WORLD WAS VERY UPSETTING TO ME. I THOUGHT I HAD DONE A GREAT DEED WHILE HELPING SOMEONE GO STRAIGHT AND HAVE A DECENT LIFE. THIS HURT TOO THE BONE AND IT STILL HURTS TO THINK I HAD BECOME CLOSE TO SOMEONE WHILE DOING A GOOD DEED FOR HIM AND SOCIETY.

THE PROBLEM WITH REFORM IS SOME KIND OOF TEMPTATION THAT PULLS A PERSON BACK INTO THE JAWS OF HELL AND CONTINUALLY HAVING A HOLD ON THEM WITH A GRIP THAT WANT LET GO.

SOME PEOPLE ARE RELEASED FROM THE GRIPS OF HELL AND GO ON TO HAVE A GOOD LIFE, BUT MANY WILL NEVER COMPLY WITH THE NORMS OF SOCIETY THAT DICTATE HOW A PERSON MUST ACT TO AVOID BEING INCARCERATED.

BUT THIS IS NOT TO SAY THAT WE GIVE UP ON PEOPLE. WE MUST CONTINUE TO ATTEMPT TO HELP ONE ANOTHER FOR THAT IS THE ONLY WAY MAN AND WOMAN WILL SURVIVE ON THIS PLACE WE CALL EARTH AND OUR HOME.

SADLY, THIS AIN'T NO DOG.

AFTER LIVING IN THE AREA FOR A FEW YEARS AN OLDER MAN CAME TO MY HOUSE ONE DAY AND INTRODUCED HIMSELF TO ME AND TOLD ME HE LIVED JUST DOWN THE ROAD FROM ME. WE TALKED FOR A WHILE AND HE TOLD ME IF I EVER NEEDED ANYONE TO HELP DO ANY KIND OF WORK TO LET HIM KNOW. I TOLD HIM I WOULD. AND AS HE LEFT, I BEGIN TO THINK OF MANY THINGS I WANTED TO DO AROUND MY HOUSE THAT I COULDN'T DO BY MYSELF. SO, I CALLED THE OLDER MAN THE NEXT DAY AND ASK HIM IF HE WAS READY TO WORK AND HE SAID YES, HE WOULD BE TO MY HOUSE IN ABOUT 15 MINUTES.

WHEN HE ARRIVED AT MY HOUSE HE BEGAN TO TALK MORE AS WE WORKED CUTTING SOME BRUSH IN BACK OF THE HOUSE. HE SAID HIS WIFE HAD DIED ABOUT A YEAR AGO AND HE NEEDED SOMETHING TO KEEP HIM BUSY WHILE TRYING TO GET OVER THE HURT.

THIS OLDER MAN WAS ABOUT 10 YEARS OLDER THAN ME AND COULD WORK MUCH HARDER THAN I COULD. I HAD TO MAKE HIM SLOW DOWN. I WAS AFRAID HE WOULD HURT HIMSELF, HAVE A HEART ATTACK OR STROKE OR SOMETHING. WHEN I FINALLY GOT HIM TO SLOW DOWN, HE STILL PERFORMED VERY FAST WHILE WORKING AT HIS JOB.

I ASK THE OLDER MAN WHY HE HAD NEVER FOUND ANOTHER WOMAN AS A COMPANION AND HE SAID HE JUST COULDN'T GET OVER HIS WIFE'S DEATH. BUT ALL THAT CHANGED FOR THE WORST WHEN HE MET A GIRL ABOUT 35 YEARS YOUNGER THAN HIM.

HE WAS GETTING GAS AT A NEARBY STORE WHEN THIS GIRL APPROACHED HIM AND ASK TO BORROW MONEY TO BUY HER CIGARETTES. SHE WAS VERY PRETTY AND WORE CLOTHES LEAVING NOTHING TOO THE IMAGINATION OF HER BODY. AND SHE WAS VERY FLIRTY TO HIM AS HE STATED. SHE WENT AS FAR AS TO HUG HIM TIGHTLY WHEN HE BOUGHT HER CIGARETTES.

HE INVITED HER TO COME TO HIS HOUSE AND SEE HIM. THE NEXT DAY SHE SHOWED UP AT HIS HOUSE AND BEGAN FLIRTING WITH HIM AGAIN. AND THIS LED TO MORE ENCOUNTERS AS TIME WENT ON. SHE ENTICED HIM TO THE POINT OF HAVING SEX

AND HE TOOK THIS AS HER CARING FOR HIM. LITTLE DID HE KNOW WHAT LAY AHEAD AS SHE MOVED IN HIS HOUSE WITH HIM.

THE GIRL, AS HE FOUND OUT HAD A VERY BAD CRIMINAL BACKGROUND AND AS TIME WENT ON HE FOUND HIMSELF SPENDING ALL OF HIS SAVINGS ON HER FOR ATTORNEYS AND OTHER LEGAL ASSISTANCE. AS HE TOLD ME HE AND HIS DECEASED WIFE HAD SAVED NEARLY TWO HUNDRED THOUSAND DOLLARS TO USE AS A RETIREMENT FUNDS. AND ALL THIS WAS GONE IN LESS THAN A YEAR. HE FOUND HIMSELF NEARLY BROKE AND BARELY MAKING ENDS MEET DUE TO THE DECEIVING FEMALE WHO CAME INTO HIS LIFE AT A TIME WHEN HE WAS VERY VULNERABLE AND IN NEED OF SOMEONE TO HAVE A LIFE WITH. NEEDLESS TO SAY, THIS GIRL WHO HAD DECEIVED HIM ENDED UP GETTING 20 YEARS IN PRISON.

AT A TIME, THE OLDER GENT HAD LOST HIS WIFE, HIS MONEY AND THE CROOKED GIRL WHO HAD TAKEN EVERYTHING FROM HIM HE WENT INSANE AND WAS PLACED IN AN INTENSIVE CARE NURSING HOME WHERE HE DIED IN LESS THAN A YEAR LATER.

WHILE THIS WAS A SAD ENDING FOR THE OLDER MAN WHO HAD BEEN FOOLED BY A DECEIVING PERSON WHO DID NOT CARE AT ALL WHAT SHE INFLICTED ON HIM. IT INDEED SHOULD SEND A WARNING TO THOSE WHO ARE VULNERABLE TO SOMEONE WHO WOULD TAKE ADVANTAGE OF THEM.

THIS AIN'T NO DOG, BUT IT IS A SAD ENDING.

THE END

AUTHOR CLYDE E. SPARKS IS FROM THE TAZEWELL COUNTY AREA OF SOUTHWEST VIRGINIA. WHILE NOW RESIDING IN THE NEWBERN, VIRGINIA, AREA IN A ONE HUNDRED AND SIXTY YEAR OLD HOUSE NAMED STONEHENGE. THE HOUSE WAS BUILT BY CIVIL WAR GENERAL JAMES ALEXANDER WALKER KNOWN AS "STONEWALL JIM" WALKER. SPARKS HAS TAUGHT CRIMINAL JUSTICE IN MULTIPLE COLLEGES. HE HOLDS TWO ASSOCIATES,' A BACHELORS, MASTERS, AND A PHD IN CRIMINAL JUSTICE, LAW AND SAFETY ENGINEERING AND CERTIFICATES FROM STATE AND FEDERAL AGENCIES.

Made in the USA
Columbia, SC
04 October 2023

23721617R10024